Clash of the the Agnivores

Books by Pat Anderson

Clash
of the
Agnivores

THE BIG LIE AND ITS
CONSEQUENCES

Pat Anderson

Snowy Publications MMXVII

First published 2014
This edition 2017

ISBN: 1499747799
ISBN-13: 978-1499747799

Dedicated to Shaun Dillon, who suggested I write this book.

And to Mick, at Bampots Utd, for his unstinting support.

Contents

Contents

Preface

Over the last couple of years there have been many blogs, including my own, about what happened, and is still happening, at Ibrox. I started my blog because I was sick to the back teeth of Jim Traynor and his blatant two-facedness when it came to Rangers. He would voice his opinion about one team and then perform a complete *volte-face* when speaking about Rangers. Challenging him on the Daily Record forums was a waste of time; I doubt he even read them. A waste of time also was calling his 'Phone-In' on Radio Scotland. At best you'd be cut off, at worst you'd be accused of being psychologically disturbed.

His partisan pieces in the Daily Record in the latter half of 2012 would make any right-thinking individual want to spew. Not only that, his downright lies and attacks on all and sundry made me angry and I knew I wasn't the only one. Somebody needed to answer the bastard back and show him up for all the crap he was being allowed to publish in the name of journalism.

Then I discovered blogging. I could vent my spleen as much as I wanted and, hopefully, others would read it, enjoy it and perhaps agree with me. And so 'Jabba The Agnivore' was born. For the first year or so I usually got under a hundred hits a day. I assumed my readers were just composed of the casually curious but was surprised to find that I had a regular band of followers. I very rarely got comments on my blog but my regular readers made the odd contribution, agreeing with me or pointing out something I had missed.

One of my earliest readers was Shaun Dillon (posting as shaun bhoy). He enjoyed my blog and suggested that I make a book out of my posts. Well, I haven't done that but I hope he enjoys the book nonetheless.

A few months ago Mick (I don't know his surname) featured one of my posts on his site Bampots Utd. This brought me more readers for my blog, as well as some welcome purchasers of my books! It also brought me to the attention of Celtic News Now, who started to feature my blogs on their page. My readership increased dramatically thereafter.

So a big thanks to Shaun and Mick. It's not just that I'm grateful but it's always better to have others to share the blame, the hate mail and the death threats with!

Pat Anderson
June 2014

Apologies for the state of some of the endnotes, which refuse point-blank to be moved, leaving spaces between them. Obviously, they are still legible so I eventually decided to leave them as they are.

Pat Anderson
March 2017

Introduction
City of The Dead

History is all about change, especially Social History: the extension of the vote, new opportunities for women, population growths and declines, immigration and emigration etc. It's fascinating to see how different people in the past were and to compare it with our own experiences.

But any historian worth his salt also knows that continuity is equally as important. We can look at the past and marvel at many of the strange, alien, customs they had but we are often surprised to find that some things were exactly the same as they are today.

People like continuity, even in times of massive change. Nobody wants everything to be totally different; even clinging onto some small remnant of the past can make all the difference between a frightening, uncertain existence and the feeling that everything is still okay.

The Reformation, for example, was one of the biggest changes that people in Europe had ever seen. Almost overnight in some places all the old certainties were thrown out of the window, to be replaced by a completely different way of looking at how religion worked. It's often seen as an exciting time but, to many, it must have been frightening as well as they struggled to make sense of being told that a way of life they had taken for granted for years was no longer relevant. In such circumstances people were bound to take comfort in elements that remained the same.

One thing that didn't change for most folk was that they still went to the same church building. It might have changed dramatically on the inside but it was still the same place. Any nagging doubts you had about this new-fangled way of worshipping could be assuaged somewhat by the knowledge that you were still in what had always been 'God's house'.

And there was still somebody up in front, haranguing you and telling you how you should live your life. He might be banging on about things you didn't understand, like Justification by Faith or the predestined salvation of the Elect, but that made no difference. The things he was telling you to do and not to do were pretty much the same things that the priest used to say.

Then there were the things that the new Church might frown on but that people clung to nonetheless. Superstitious folk in Germany, deprived of their saints, used to hang a picture of Martin Luther up to ward off evil and keep the family safe. Meanwhile Calvin and Knox might demand to be buried in unmarked graves but the rich and powerful in Geneva and Scotland weren't going to be denied their extravagant memorials, even inside the church buildings.

As well as a need for continuity people like to look back to the past as a time when things were better. Nowadays folk are nostalgic for the good old days of the Nineteen-Fifties; but people back then were just the same. At a time when Rock and Roll singers were screeching out of the radio, Teddy Boys were smashing up cinemas and black people were 'flooding in' from the Caribbean, folk looked back with nostalgia to the days of the war, when everybody pulled together. This was despite the fact that during the war rapes, murders, muggings and burglaries were at an all-time high.

Those in power that are leading changes also tend to couch the changes in terms of a return to some halcyon past. Hitler painted Nazi Germany as a return to the days of the Teutonic Knights, while Communism is all about going back to some distant past where there was no demarcation of labour. Even during the Reformation, it was said that they were returning the Church to where it had been in its infancy.

All these tendencies came into play with The People. They longed for the good old days of nine-in-a-row, when Rangers dominated Scottish football. This hearkening for the past was made all the more powerful by the fact that things actually *were* better in the old days. Now there was nothing but uncertainty and fear.

Craig Whyte had sold the Arsenal shares and buggered off on the St Etienne Bike, leaving a tangled mess behind him. After a drawn-out administration the inevitable happened: liquidation. That was it – Rangers was dead. All that was left was Charles Green, who picked up the keys to Ibrox from the administrators, Duff and Phelps. And so a new club started.

Of course, The People would follow this new club; it would be playing at Ibrox and Green had promised that Sevco would be changed to The Rangers. It was a huge wrench, however, and, as at any point in history, The People groped around for signs of continuity.

And then the whispering began; it wasn't a new club at all. It was still Rangers. The club was separate from the company, which had been left for the liquidators to deal with. In no time at all this whispering became a defiant crescendo and so the Big Lie came into being. And that is what this book is about; the Big Lie and its consequences.

Consequences? Well, there were bound to be some. We all expected legal challenges and the football authorities to accept none of this shite, but the shite continued uncontested. The powers-that-be, along with our media, helped promulgate the myth and The People looked upon it and saw that it was good. Amen.

But there were other consequences to the Big Lie. The main one was that nagging doubt in the back of everyone's mind: was this really Rangers, the same team, the same club? After all, who was Charles Green? Who was Imran Ahmad? Who was Brian Stockbridge? Nobody had ever heard of them before and they certainly weren't what you would call 'Real Rangers Men'.

Bits of continuity had been okay to cling to during the days of the Reformation; after all, Protestantism was being hailed as a new church, or, rather, the reinstitution of an ancient one. Some things remained the same, as outlined above, to make the transition easier. The same thing could have been true if it had been accepted that Green's club was a new one. But now that it had been heralded that it was still Rangers, rather more continuity was required than just a name, a stadium and a strip.

The nostalgia for the good old days combined with the need for continuity to produce a desire, a hunger, to make Green's club into Rangers again. The only way that was going to be done would be to get 'Real Rangers Men,' men that had been around during the David Murray glory days, back in charge. Green was now surplus to requirements.

Even amid the initial hailing of Charles Green as a saviour, there was always that note of disapproval. In fact, Green was hardly in the door before moves were made to get rid of him. He was not what either The People or the media envisaged as a suitable person to run 'Rangers'.

In Ancient Rome when there was a crisis, like a war that wasn't going too well, the Senate would appoint a 'dictator' to take charge during the emergency. The dictator's word was law and he had power over the army as well as the civil government. Once the crisis was over, however, the dictator was expected to stand down and duly-elected officials to take charge once more. Any dictator that tried to hold onto power would soon find a knife sliding into his back as he entered the Senate House.

Green was viewed like one of these 'dictators' of old. Yes, he had done his bit and 'Rangers had been saved' but the crisis was over now so he was no longer needed. It was time for him to piss off and for things at Ibrox to get back to business as usual.

I spoke of doubts and they were there, just below the surface. The People might shout about 'unbroken history' and 'continuity' but, in reality, the only continuity was manifested in Sooperally and a handful of players that knew nobody else would want them. More continuity was needed and that meant 'Real Rangers Men'. 'Real Rangers Men' at Ibrox = 'Real Rangers'.

Right from the start Green was on a hiding to nothing. It wouldn't have mattered if he'd succeeded in getting his new club into the SPL, brought in rich investors with deep pockets and was making money hand-over-fist; he wasn't a 'Real Rangers Man'. All the accusations flung at Green and his heirs were rationalisations, ways of justifying the general disapproval of them. The actual reasons for wanting them out were there if you looked for them.

Rationalisations are normal practice as far as The People are concerned. Look at the way they all hate Neil Lennon. Ask them why and they'll tell you it's because he's a whinger, a moaner, a ned, a thug etc etc. These are rationalizations; made-up reasons for disguising prejudice. They'll say, 'Look at how aggressive he is in the dugout!' But they hated him before he became manager. 'But he was a ned on the pitch.' Was he? Not that I can remember. They'll supply examples but with each instance they bring up it can easily be shown that their hatred preceded it. They'll never admit to the real reason for their hatred, though.

The given reasons for wanting rid of people on the Ibrox board are just rationalisations as well. Every new face was welcomed, not with relief or positivity, but with hatred and mistrust. Look at how the appointment of Craig Mather was received, or Graham Wallace or David Somers. And look who they wanted to replace them with!

I have tried as much as possible to provide sources for my narrative, so the reader can check for him or herself the evidence available. There might be the odd case where the reader thinks I've missed out some pieces of evidence, remembering so-and-so saying such-and-such. There are many things I remembered, or thought I remembered, as I was writing this but I stuck to one basic principle: if I couldn't provide a source then I wouldn't include it. Thankfully there were very few occasions where this dilemma arose.

This, of course, meant that the book took longer than I thought it would to write. It's been a long time since I left university but I'd still like to think that I can approach a topic like this as a historian and that my old tutors wouldn't find too much fault with how I've presented my argument.

I have avoided discussing the bigotry still on display at Ibrox, except where it is essential to my central theme; for example, I have not discussed the bigoted singing at the Armed Forces Day in 2013 since this has nothing to do with my theme. The Armed Forces Day of 2012, however, is a different matter as it was part of Charles Green's concerted effort to ingratiate himself with The People. This book is not an exercise in dissecting the anachronistic views of The People; that has been done many times before. Nor is it a look at how Rangers died; Phil Mac Giolla Bhain has already covered that ground in his book 'Downfall'.

My interest is in how the Big Lie, that Rangers didn't die and is still in existence, impacted upon those that believed it and promulgated it. The Big Lie became more important than players, directors and even more important than the club itself. The need for 'Real Rangers Men' in situ to preserve the Big Lie meant that many in the support would rather the club went to the wall completely than entrust it to those they deemed unsuitable.

You will already have noticed that I'm employing an informal, almost chatty style in this book. For example, I'm using abbreviations like 'I'm' instead of 'I am' and words like 'pish' and 'shite,' both words that I'm rather fond of using. I didn't want to end up with some dry historical treatise. I have tried to balance my instincts as a historian, striving for accuracy, while at the same time remembering that this is not a PhD thesis; I actually want people to buy it! Hopefully I have succeeded and folk find the book entertaining and enjoyable as well as informative and providing some food for thought.

I make no apology in concentrating on the blogs of Bill McMurdo and David Leggat. Both these bloggers were of one mind in 2012 but as time went on their viewpoints became further and further apart. Each of them represents an opposite side in the 'Real Rangers Men' war and it was mainly their websites that told the story of either side.

In case anyone is looking at the notes and is not familiar with the term 'ibid,' it simply means that it's the same as the one beforehand. (It's short for the Latin 'ibidem' meaning 'in the same place.) It's just to save having to write (or type) out the same title again.

The term 'Op. Cit.' means that the name of the work, in this case the website, has already been given.

Since all my sources are online I have omitted a bibliography. The sources in the notes are self-explanatory and don't need any expansion.

I have also not included an index. This is quite a short book and so it should be quite easy to find what you're looking for without recourse to an index. Now *that's* what you call a rationalisation! The real reason for not including an index is that I'm a lazy bastard and couldn't be bothered making one!

I had intended ending my book with the AGM in December 2013 but the themes I outline are ongoing. It might be difficult to know where, exactly, to stop but it's easy to know where to begin. Let's meet Charles Green in happier times, when he was entering the New Jerusalem of Govan with The People shouting 'Hosanna' and strewing his path with palm leaves as he rode in on a donkey called Lee McCulloch.

Clash of the Agnivores

1

Complete Control

Church bells rang out all over the world as the joyful news spread. Spontaneous street parties broke out on every continent while some folk just stood, tearful, overcome with emotion. It was like the Berlin Wall coming down, Nelson Mandela being released and the end of the Second World War all rolled into one. Rangers had been saved! Charles Green had arrived in the nick of time and prevented 140 years of history being flushed down the crapper.

Well, that's the story we were fed by our esteemed Fourth Estate but it didn't quite happen like that. In reality a tawdry, backstairs deal was done between Green and the administrators, Duff and Phelps before the liquidators arrived. Green picked up the assets for a song, while a cock-and-bull story about holding companies was broadcast to justify Green's claim that it was the 'same club'. In the process hundreds of creditors were shafted out of the money they were due, including the local paper shop.

If things were as simple as that it begs the question as to why the club was in administration so long. What was the point in trying to find buyers with huge bank accounts? What was the point in proposing CVAs? The whole thing could have been done and dusted within a couple of days of going into administration. The only problem with that is that Duff and Phelps wouldn't have earned anywhere near as much as they did.

Our agnivores in the press were ready, just like Sooperally, to give their support to anyone. In April they had been all over Bill Ng like a rash, telling us how he had had a 'lifelong passion' for Rangers ever since he had seen them winning the European Cup-Winners' Cup back in 1972.[1] Strangely enough, Craig Whyte had been fired by the same passion; or so we were told. Wiser heads pointed out that Ng's proposals didn't quite add up. He seemed to think that £20m was going to be enough and there were doubts that he had enough money to do all the things he said he was going to. Eventually he pulled out, blaming Duff and Phelps for their intransigence.[2]

Then we had Bill Miller, with his mad scheme of playing hide-and-seek with the assets.[3] This was another guy with 'wealth off the radar' and our press was again all over him. The Daily Record even told us how his beauty-queen wife was going to be the 'First Lady of Ibrox'.[4]

The Rangers Supporters Trust denounced Miller's plans,[5] which involved putting the assets into a newco, letting Duff and Phelps try to get a CVA for Rangers and then amalgamating the newco with Rangers when everything was alright again. The danger with this was that Rangers might be liquidated and all that would be left would be a new club. Miller ended up pulling out, with the opposition of the fans being a major reason.

So everybody accepted that liquidation meant the death of Rangers; anything that came after would be a new club. So when Rangers did, eventually, die there was an air of resignation about the whole thing. They had come to half expect that their club wasn't going to make it. Now here was somebody, in fact a lot of folk, telling them that their club hadn't died at all. They couldn't believe their good fortune! The Rangers support, including those in the media, were only too willing to swallow this story whole.

Of course, it wasn't all plain sailing for Green at first. Sooperally was ready at one point to 'do walking away' when he apparently discovered that Green wanted rid of him. A 'source' said about Sooper, 'Honesty, dignity and courage have always been the driving forces in McCoist's make-up but he doesn't think those qualities have been in abundance outwith the players, staff and fans.'[6]

This was going to create major problems for Green. Sooperally had become a hero to The People and was the only link left with the old club. Getting rid of Sooper would mean an uphill climb in pretending that Green's club was 'still Rangers'. He also faced a threat to try to oust him, even though he had only just got himself ensconced in the Blue Room.

A consortium, made up of Douglas Park, described as 'the bus tycoon,' Jim McColl, the owner of Clyde Blowers and Walter Smith made plain their intention to buy Green out.[7] This was going to be a formidable force to contend with, especially given Smith's iconic status. Green said that he'd sell for £20m, which he knew this bunch would never come up with.[8] Sooperally was bound to give this group his support, which meant that Green would be hard-pushed to sell even one season ticket.

It was obvious whose side our media was on. Yes, Green had saved Rangers but he wasn't a 'Real Rangers Man,' was he? It was a case of, 'Thank you very much for saving Rangers. Now fuck off!'

The People voiced their support for Smith and his gang, while the Rangers Supporters Trust called for a season-ticket boycott to starve Green out. Green was in an unusually conciliatory mood and offered to make Smith chairman of his new club. He said, 'If Walter Smith wants to ring me, wants to meet me, wants me to go to his house, I'll do it.'[9]

When it came to the crunch Smith's millionaires shit themselves and pulled out. Green, and his backer Zeus Capital, even offered to let the millionaires come in with them but, instead, they stormed off in the huff. Green was now the undisputed master at Ibrox.[10] He also managed to get Sooperally onside. Sooper said that he had decided to stay because 'The most important thing is the future of my club.'[11] It would be over a year before we discovered the real reason for Sooper's change of heart. Suffice it to say that Scotland's pie manufacturers never had it so good.

Since Green was the last man standing, and Sooperally was now on his side, the Rangers fans flocked to buy season tickets; something they thought they might never be able to do again. Charles Green went among them, giving out cups of tea and wee bottles of ginger for the weans. This, of course, went down well but not half as well as his belligerent language as he promised to 'stand oop' to the football authorities. A quick visit to East Belfast didn't do him any harm either.

And so began the myth of Charles Green saving Rangers. Green played up to this fully, especially when it came to the investigation of the side letters by Lord Nimmo-Smith, acting on behalf of the SFA. Nobody was going to take titles away from Rangers, he maintained. They had an unbroken 140-year history, he said. Everybody's got it in for them, he said. This was all mother's milk, of course, to The People.

Our newspapers joined in, using words like 'relegated' to describe where Green's Neo-Gers were in the league. In reality, of course, Scottish football, especially the supporters, weren't going to stand by and see this new team shoe-horned into the SPL. Why should this club get any special favours? In truth, the new club shouldn't even have been allowed into the leagues at all; there were other clubs in front of it in the queue. Even letting Neo-Gers into Division 3 was bending over backwards to accommodate them. The People, however, and their cheerleaders in the press, saw things differently.

Since Green's club was still Rangers then there shouldn't have been any argument about it. A points deduction for 'a second insolvency event' and that should have been it. This was 'Scotland's biggest club' we were talking about; how dare they treat it this way! Obviously Green was right; everybody had it in for his club.

Leading the good fight was one James Sexton Traynor; affectionately known as Jabba to his readers and listeners. In a complete and utter show of sheer brass neck, he went back on his previous statements of Rangers being dead[12] to become the main cheerleader of Green's 'Same Team' agenda.

Of course, it did not matter in the slightest if none of the rest of us bought into the Big Lie that this club was 'still Rangers'. After all, none of us were ever going to buy season tickets or merchandise, were we? This campaign was aimed squarely at The People and, more specifically, their wallets.

Jabba conjured up different bogeymen that had 'nearly' destroyed Rangers. HMRC was the first. Incredibly, he expected us all to believe that Her Majesty's tax inspectors went after Rangers out of sheer hatred and bigotry. David Murray had offered a settlement, but no; HMRC had to see it through to the bitter end.[13]

Then we had the SFA and the SPL. They should have listened to Jabba. How could Scottish football in general, and, more specifically, the SPL, survive without Rangers? After all, Rangers was the biggest club in the universe, spreading financial largesse to all the lesser teams. Armageddon was coming and it was all the fault of the SPL for 'relegating' Rangers and the SFA for standing by and allowing this to happen.

But the biggest bogeyman of all was Craig Whyte; after all, Rangers went into administration on his watch. Jabba started to say that Rangers' debt had been reduced to a manageable level before Whyte came on the scene.[14] He even went on a BBC programme blaming Whyte for everything, coming out with the classic line, 'I've been saying this all along!'

In fact, he had been saying nothing of the kind. In 2010 he went on and on about how the 'Lifelong Light Blues fan' was coming to plough millions into the club. In June 2011 he was talking about 'front-loaded war chests,' whatever the hell that means. This cash was going to be 'ring-fenced' and more would be available if Sooperally needed it.

Now, however, in late 2012, Whyte was Satan incarnate. Of course, blaming Craig Whyte let Jabba's god, the divine David Murray, who dispensed succulent lamb to the chosen, off the hook. Partaking of the Agnus Davi, however, came at a high cost. You were entering into a sacred covenant, where you had to give over your life to protecting your god. It's like one of those strange, American cults.

Green seemed to be the new messiah, carrying on where Murray had left off. Whyte had done his best to destroy Rangers but had failed. Things were going to get back to normal, while all over Britain the sphincters of new-born lambs quivered in fearful anticipation.

Everybody in the press followed Jabba in slavish admiration of Green, especially praising his outspokenness and Yorkshire bluntness. Jabba's old friend, David Leggat, he of the Presbyterian granny, took time out from his eternal, one-sided feud with Graham Spiers to say how wonderful Green was. Not only that, but Green's associates, like Imran Ahmad and Brian Stockbridge, were the best things that had ever happened at Ibrox and they were more than suitable as custodians of the Neo-Gers, or Rangers, as many would have us believe.[15]

Only one discordant note was sounded. A baldy ex-Rangers player stood on the steps at Ibrox, dressed in his dad's ill-fitting, old demob suit, and shouted, 'Showzzideeds!' Whose name was on them? In the general feeling of overwhelming joy, however, his protestations were completely ignored.

Of course, when it came to the practicalities of Neo-Gers' existence, the Big Lie had no place. There was trepidation over whether the team would be able to play at all; it was not registered with the SFA as a club. Our great leaders, however, were ready to ride to the rescue. A temporary licence was issued, an unprecedented act, to allow the Neo-Gers to play their first league game against Peterhead. Afterwards, the licence of Rangers was transferred over to the Neo-Gers. Surely this wouldn't have been necessary if it was still the same club?

On the field things were not that great. Neo-Gers' very first match in Division 3 ended in a draw against Peterhead. After that things did not get much better as any wins they did get were by a very slender margin and often the result of a penalty or the opposition being reduced to ten men. This lack of quality, however, was put down to Sooperally having to cope with a depleted squad. Things were bound to pick up.

Green huffed and puffed about the players that left after liquidation. According to him, those players should have remained at Ibrox under TUPE regulations. These regulations, however, only apply if the company, in this case Rangers, is actually taken over. Green did nothing more than buy the assets but it is testament to the work of himself and his supporters in the media that he evidently believed that he had taken over, and saved, Rangers. Nobody, except the usual 'internet bampots' tried to disabuse him of this fantasy.

As to Sooperally's squad, the transfer embargo imposed on Neo-Gers, rather conveniently, did not come into effect until the transfer window was closed. Sooper had the same amount of time as every other manager to suss out players and he did sign a couple from the SPL. The press still insisted, however, in calling the Neo-Gers team 'kids' and in claiming that Sooperally was playing with a vastly depleted squad.

A huge boost for the Big Lie came in December when the European Club Association let Green's club remain within it, albeit as associate members. It was a strange business, though. The ECA is based at UEFA Headquarters in Nyon, Switzerland. Under Swiss law, 'membership of an association is neither heritable nor transferable'.[16] So Neo-Gers had to apply for membership. There was a stumbling block, though; members had to be in their country's top division and have a UEFA club licence. It looked as if their application would be refused.

The weird thing was that the ECA then stated, 'Taking into account that the 'new entity' also acquired the goodwill of the 'old entity', it was held by the ECA executive board that the goodwill, taking into account legal and practical arguments, also included the history of the 'old company'.[17] Effectively, the ECA decided that Green's club was Rangers, since it had inherited all the history. Since all founder members of the ECA, of which Rangers had been one, were guaranteed automatic membership. Green's club, therefore, was allowed in, called Rangers and was treated as if it was still the old club. Their associate membership meant that Neo-Gers was not allowed to vote on any issues.

It's a tricky business all this stuff about history. When you're ready to graduate from university, having completed three or four years of study, you have to apply to receive your degree; they don't just hand it over automatically. You actually have to apply to the University Bursar's office so they can check to see if you owe them any money. If you do, and you don't pay up then you ain't getting your degree. You can argue till you're blue in the face but no money, no degree.

Effectively all the history of your time at university means nothing. Who's going to give you a job when you don't have a degree certificate to prove what you've been studying and how you did in your exams? The money you owe to the university is part of your university history. You have to accept all of your history; you can't just cherry pick which bits suit you.

Surely the same should apply to football teams. Yes, I know businesses liquidate and start over all the time, shafting creditors left, right and centre, but very few would be stupid enough to claim to be the same company. If any did, they would be liable for the debts of the old company. Green appeared to be getting away with claiming to be the same in some circumstances, but different in others. If his club was inheriting the history of the old club, then surely that should include its debts? Obviously the rules, not to mention the law, were being bent almost to breaking point just to accommodate this one club.

There was a huge degree of double standards at play too in the ECA decision. If Green's club was still Rangers, one of the founding members of the ECA, then why did it have to apply for membership? Nobody, however, was interested in answering these questions; probably because they couldn't. To The People and their friends in the media, however, this acceptance by the ECA was nothing short of a triumph.

Meanwhile, opposition to the Big Lie was jumped on and squashed. First we had the craven capitulation of The Sun. Phil Mac Giolla Bhain's book, 'Downfall,' had already caused ructions in book stores, where staff were openly threatened for stocking it. The Sun newspaper (I use the term loosely) carried an interview with Mac Giolla Bhain, telling how his life was under threat. The paper then proposed to serialise the book, relating 'How Rangers self-destructed'. Cue all the angry phone calls, e-mails and threats to The Sun.

Whether it was fear of violence, or straightforward fear of a circulation drop, The Sun caved in and decided not to go ahead with the serialisation. They gave as a reason the supposed fact that Mac Giolla Bhain was 'tarred with the brush of sectarianism.'[18] They didn't bother, of course, to mention who had been wielding the brush.

And so a major voice of dissent was silenced. David Leggat was overjoyed and lost no time in telling The People just what he thought of Phil Mac Giolla Bhain. His Presbyterian granny had no doubt been turning in her grave at the thought of one of *them* being given a platform in a newspaper!

There was one minor problem that still had to be fixed: The Daily Record online forum. Day after day there was all manner of racist and bigoted posts on this forum; words like Fenian, Taig, Tarrier and Papes were used without any censorship or censure. At the weekend all posts by Celtic supporters were mysteriously deleted, while those of The People were allowed to stand, no matter what they said. The Daily Record IT staff claimed that they were being hacked but they hardly moved Heaven and Earth to fix the problem.

The major cause for concern was what the paper called, 'personal abuse' directed against 'members of our staff.' I never saw any such abuse. What I did see, however, was the staff being exposed as hypocrites. Jabba was constantly reminded of his assertion that Rangers had died; a fact that he seemed to have conveniently forgotten. Also, whenever any Daily Record writer started banging on about the 'evil' Craig Whyte, the terms 'wealth off the radar,' 'frontloaded war chests' and 'lifelong Rangers-supporting billionaire' were cast up in their faces. Obviously this couldn't be permitted to go on.

And so, on the 13th October 2012 the Daily Record decided that it would no longer allow comments on its football stories. Thus the opposition to the Big Lie was being systematically wiped out and being forced to become the preserve solely of the 'Internet Bampot'.

Meanwhile, Charles Green's lashing out at all and sundry had caught up with him and he was hauled up before the SFA for bringing the game into disrepute. The evidence was there for all to see; his interviews on the television and in the newspapers, where he called everyone bigots and even questioned the integrity of Lord Nimmo-Smith. Incredibly, the SFA decided to find the case against Green Not Proven.

A 'Not Proven' verdict means neither innocent nor guilty; Jabba, however, proclaimed Green 'cleared of all charges.' He also said that Green was now being more conciliatory. Green showed this by issuing one of his usual threats. 'Perhaps it is time that those people within the SPL who have been pursuing Rangers at every turn take stock.'[19]

The whole affair was a fiasco and, if anything, showed that the Neo-Gers were going to be handled with the same kid gloves as Rangers always had been. This would help in the promotion of the idea that Rangers had never died and were still around. Of course, having

Campbell Ogilvie EBT as president of the SFA couldn't hurt either!

So Green was allowed to carry on his merry way, accusing everybody of having it in for his club, while Jabba cheered him on from the sidelines. The official Daily Record line was now that Rangers were still around, Green was right about everything and anyone that said differently was a bigot.

If Green had taken the time to take a good look at what had been going on around him, however, instead of getting caught up in all the nonsense, he might have planned a bit better for the future. The supporters, and the agnivores in the media, were ready to turn on him at the drop of a hat. He was playing a dangerous game. He might have been better off admitting that his was a new team and starting from scratch instead of going for the fast buck. He was not a 'Real Rangers Man' and never would be. There were plenty of those that were, and who would be only too willing to stab him in the back.

2
What's My Name?

The time that everybody had been anticipating was nearly upon us. The First Tier Tax Tribunal would be publishing its findings on The Big Tax Case. Incredibly, many supporters and journalists were pushing the line that Rangers had not yet been found guilty of anything. 'Innocent until proven guilty,' was the argument being spouted. This ignored the fact that the FTTT was actually an appeal court; Rangers had already been found guilty and had appealed the decision.

As we were constantly being told, the FTTT was exactly what it said on the tin: a first tier. If and when the case against Rangers was upheld, then they were still free to appeal further. This, of course, would be what Rangers would do when the expected result was made public. Who would be doing the appealing, however, was unclear. Would it be Charles Green on behalf of the 'same club'? Would it be BDO, the liquidators, on behalf of the 'old holding company'? It was going to be interesting to see.

Jabba, of course, saw the whole thing as nothing more than a witch hunt. Rather naïvely, or, more likely, disingenuously, he pointed out that Employee Benefits Trusts were not illegal when they were used at Rangers.[1] He was quite right; they weren't. What was illegal, however, was using them as part of an employee's normal salary. This was what HMRC was claiming had happened at Rangers. The EBTs weren't being used as any kind of reward or bonus, which was perfectly acceptable, but as part of players' contracted wages. This is what HMRC had to prove to show that Rangers had used the scheme as a way of evading taxes.

The Rangers Tax Case blog had for ages been telling us how the investigation was going. Nearly every day we learned something new that sealed Rangers' doom. And doomed they undoubtedly were. Even The People had come to accept that eventuality. They didn't bother arguing that the First Tier Tribunal would come to any other conclusion, instead pointing fingers at Celtic and saying, 'What aboot Juninho?'

And then the results were finally published. To the astonishment of everyone, the tribunal found mostly in favour of Rangers. It was not a unanimous decision; one of the three members completely disagreed with the other two. It was a strange decision to say the least and it may well be that the tribunal had one eye on what had happened to Phil Mac Giolla Bhain, The Sun newspaper and others. Fear can be a powerful incentive.

The dissenting judge was of the opinion that the EBT money received by employees constituted earnings and should be taxed. The other two, however, maintained that the moneys were actually loans and could be recovered from each person's estate. There were question marks over a few payments and they should be subject to tax but nowhere near the amount claimed by HMRC.[2]

Anybody that's ever signed on the dole, even during the summer holidays, will remember the question on the form: are you owed money by anyone? And if you apply to make yourself bankrupt, I've no doubt that the same question would be asked. Somebody owing you money is an asset to be liquidated. This should mean a lot of skid-marked y-fronts as BDO try to recover all this money owed to Rangers; the fact that there are not shows that there are double standards at play here.

Over £47m was handed out in EBT 'loans'. That sum would pay off all the creditors in one fell swoop. Even the face painter could get what's owed to her. But there have been no indications of this happening. So when it comes to tax, the payments were loans but when it comes to paying them back then they're regarded as outright gifts, although the side letters would suggest otherwise. In effect the whole thing was, and still is, one big con. Surely the judges could see that? Unless, as I said earlier, they were too scared to reach a proper judgment!

Whatever the reason behind the decision it was, of course, hailed as a victory by all connected with Ibrox. Jabba, especially, saw it as a complete vindication and proof of his contention that HMRC had acted unreasonably, prompted by hatred and bigotry. Like Sooperally, he demanded to know names and suggested that the police should be looking into those that were in charge of the whole

11

investigation into EBTs. Never mind going after the tax dodgers; it was the tax authorities that should be under scrutiny!

He then demanded that HMRC drop the whole thing. What was the point in appealing the decision and going after a 'dead' company? If they did appeal, then it only served to prove his point that they were out to get Rangers no matter what.[3]

Bill McMurdo, a prominent Rangers blogger, hailed it as one in the eye for all the Rangers haters. He said it made Phil Mac Giolla Bhain's book a work of fiction and made Alex Thomson a clown. It was a vindication of David Murray and meant that the liquidation had been totally unnecessary. He predicted lawyers' letters being sent out to everybody that had called David Murray and Rangers cheats.[4]

Jabba also questioned the point of the current SPL investigation into double contracts and side letters at Rangers. Now that Rangers had been cleared of all charges then the only reason to continue with this investigation was to keep persecuting Rangers.[5] Strangely, whenever anyone had suggested that our football authorities had it in for Celtic, Jabba had always accused them of being paranoid. A different story now, though!

Green also played up the paranoia angle. Nobody was going to take Rangers' title wins off them, he stated. He also claimed to be refusing to cooperate with the inquiry, since the SPL had no jurisdiction over his club, which was in the SFL.[6] But the disputed titles were won in the SPL, Charlie! Ah, but that was under a different company. Okay, so those titles belong to the old company then, don't they? Nay, lad; I bought those titles when I bought the history. But they were SPL titles nonetheless and surely the SPL has jurisdiction over them? Nay, because the SPL has no jurisdiction over a club in the SFL! But you said…oh, forget it!

And so we were privy to the sheer insanity of the whole situation. Green claimed that the SPL had no jurisdiction over his club and therefore no jurisdiction over the titles that belonged to it. But if his club was still Rangers then he had to concede that it used to be in the SPL and that the SPL had jurisdiction over previous title wins. To argue otherwise meant that it was a new club, starting over in the bottom tier. In that case it had no history to speak of at all. But Green also claimed that it was the same club, with 140 years of history. So which was it? It couldn't be both, could it?

There is a condition known as *cognitive dissonance*, which means that the sufferer undergoes great mental stress as he tries to balance a belief in two contradictory propositions. The theory says that normal humans require *consonance* to function properly and will go to any lengths to achieve it. This can result in severe mental stress. Maybe that's why many of The People are so violent! Then again, perhaps *cognitive dissonance* doesn't explain the thought processes of The People. After all, they seem to be perfectly happy with holding contrary beliefs.

George Orwell came up with a new phrase, *Doublethink*, to describe the holding of contradictory propositions to be true with no apparent ill effects. If all your peers do the same thing, then it makes it a lot easier to believe in two contrary propositions. The herd mentality means that you don't need to question either belief. Of course, it also helps if you happen to be thick!

Green tried to make sense of the whole thing by resorting to tortuous explanations. The club was simply an asset of the holding company that went into liquidation. When Green bought 'the assets' from Duff and Phelps, he effectively bought the club. This meant that he bought the business of the club and also bought its history. This, of course, caused hilarity among those that didn't feel the need to believe everything Green said. Everyone especially laughed at the idea of buying history or claiming the history of something you've acquired.

There are a lot of fit, young people these days that carry organ donor cards. I could be next in line for a heart transplant and be in luck when one becomes available. While strutting about with my nice, new heart, I discover that a young man who was Wimbledon Singles Champion has been killed in a car crash and it is his heart that I've got. Using Charles Green's logic, I can now claim to be Wimbledon Champion and demand to be seeded for next year's competition!

Or, given the way things are going with the NHS we might have to start buying prosthetic items from the families of those that have died while wearing them. I could buy some old boy's dentures, which were hand-crafted back in the 1930s. After some adjustments, and a good cleansing, by a dental laboratory, I have my own remaining stumps removed and my fine, gleaming, new choppers fitted. I could then claim to have helped liberate France, since the old boy was wearing these gnashers when he stormed a Normandy beach on D-Day!

Jabba was caught up in all this *doublethink* as well. When Whyte appeared in the press in October to answer all those deriding him, he claimed that 'Rangers' had been 'relegated' to Division 3. Jabba was quick to counter this by saying, 'Rangers had to go there because they were a new club starting over.'[7] And yet, he was constantly spouting the line that Green's club was still the same club with 140 years of history! It's enough to drive you mental trying to make sense of all this nonsense.

So let's see if I've got this straight. Rangers went into administration but the holding company went into liquidation, leaving Rangers, the club, free to start over. Now if you look at Rangers accounts from previous years there is a holding company listed: Murray International Holdings. So was that the holding company that went into liquidation? Er…no. This holding company was called The Rangers Football Club PLC. But wasn't that what the club was called?

Under company law it is illegal to separate bits of a company in order to avoid paying creditors; but this is exactly what Duff and Phelps did. The trading side of the club was separated into a 'holding company,' which they called The Rangers Football Club PLC. They renamed this phantom company RFC 2012 PLC and that's what was liquidated. The rest was sold to Charles Green for not much more than the fees due to Duff and Phelps.

Considering that this is illegal, how were they able to get away with it? Because everybody looked the other way, that's how. Nobody wanted to know about the law; all that mattered was that 'Rangers' was still around.

To keep the Big Lie going The People insisted that their club be called 'Rangers' at all times. Any deviation from this rule caused them to start crying and screeching to the heavens. Nothing less than blood would appease them.

The PA announcer at Falkirk, for example, caused a furore when he read out the scores to the crowd at Falkirk Stadium, by saying, 'Peterhead 2, Sevco Franchise 2.' Such a fuss was made that Falkirk had to apologise and the poor announcer was suspended.[8]

Later in the season Montrose had to apologise when The People took umbrage at the match programme, which said, 'Playing their first season in Division Three, The Rangers are a newco of the now defunct Glasgow Rangers. Currently top of the table, they will be hoping to go on to seal the title and clinch their first silverware.'[9] Cue the outrage from The People and Montrose having to apologise.

Just like in George Orwell's book, those that subscribed to the *doublethink* of the Big Lie wanted to make sure that everyone else would subscribe as well. No opposition would be brooked. A special Room 101 had been set aside at Hampden to deal with troublemakers!

Nobody ever bothered to explain how the whole thing worked; there was no need since the media seemed to be accepting it without question. Imagine if there had been a proper Q & A session about this, with one of the *doublethinking* People explaining how Green's club was still the same but under a different 'holding company'.

So, the 'assets, business and history' were sold to Green. But wait a minute, isn't 'business' exactly the same as 'trading'? So if Green bought the 'trading' part then doesn't that mean he bought the whole shebang?

No. He bought the assets.

If he bought the assets, then doesn't that mean that he started a new club altogether?

No. He bought the business of the old company.

So was the 'business' listed as one of the assets of Rangers Football Club PLC?

Don't be stupid. How can you list 'business' as an asset? The 'business' was the day-to-day operation of the company.

The trading?

15

Exactly.

So he bought the company then, along with its trading?

No. He didn't buy the company. He bought the assets, including the business.

So all those people that did business with the old company, who did they send the invoices to?

Rangers Football Club PLC.
And what was the name of the actual club?

Rangers Football Club.
And was Rangers Football Club listed as an asset of Rangers Football Club PLC?

No.

And yet you claim that Green bought the assets, which included Rangers Football Club. How did he manage that?

He bought the assets, which included the business of the club.

But...You know what - fuck it! Quick, let's get onto the next chapter before my brain explodes!

3
Give 'Em Enough Rope

A major component of the media's promotion of the Big Lie was that any titles that Celtic won while Neo-Gers weren't in the SPL would be 'tainted'. Mark Hateley, in his column in the Daily Record, was the main proponent of this nonsense. It was grabbed eagerly by The People and made its way onto various blogs and became an accepted maxim by many in our media.

Hateley had already gone on record as saying that Celtic's 2011/12 title was 'tainted'. This was because Rangers was attempting 'to battle for its very existence'.[1] In other words, because Rangers had been facing financial and other off-field problems, Celtic had had an easy ride.

Cast your mind back to the 1980s and 1990s, assuming you're old enough, that is! In 1988 Celtic won the SPL title in their centenary year, with a crowded (apparently overcrowded) stadium to witness the victory over Dundee United that clinched it. Celebrations abounded. Unfortunately, such celebrations were not to be seen at Celtic Park for another ten years! Celtic couldn't even manage to finish in second place until a full eight years after this title win.

Everybody knows about the money troubles at Celtic and how the club nearly disappeared in 1994, only being saved at the very last minute. Strangely, I haven't heard anyone say a word about Rangers' title that year being tainted. Celtic was attempting 'to battle for its very existence' in this period, just as Rangers was in 2012. So, using Hateley's argument, that Rangers title win should have a big asterisk next to it. Hoist with his own petard, I think the phrase is.

Back in 2012 I used to post quite regularly on the Daily Record forum. After Hateley's ridiculous article I put forward the following scenario. Remember, Motherwell had finished third in the SPL so would get the chance to qualify for the Champions League instead of Rangers, who had died.

Imagine Motherwell manages to shock everyone by getting into the group stages of the Champions League. Not only that, but they actually win their group and get into the knock-out matches. Defying all

17

expectations, they dispose of some big guns and get to face Barcelona in the final. The sense of excitement in Scotland reaches fever pitch and the whole country is behind the Steelmen.

History is made when Motherwell beat Barcelona in normal time, becoming only the second Scottish team to win the European Cup and the first to win the competition in its current format. The team is going to be a shoo-in for that year's Scottish Sports Personality of the Year and maybe even the British accolade.

Attendances at Fir Park have never been higher and the team is cheered onto the pitch everywhere it goes. The club has single-handedly restored pride in Scottish football and this has had a knock-on effect on football attendance figures overall.

A proud Tom Hateley goes to show his dad his medal. Dad takes one look at it, sneers and says, 'It's tainted!'

It was an unlikely thing to happen (and, of course, it didn't) but it illustrated the stupidity of Hateley's argument. But, then again, maybe his definition of 'tainted' only applied to Celtic and nobody else.

Hateley also said the title was 'a title they somehow failed to win throughout the last three years of financial troubles'.[2] So, he was essentially saying that the only way that Celtic could win was because Rangers went into administration. He was also regurgitating the old myth of 'Nae dough, three in a row,' which was a load of garbage since an absolute fortune was spent on players during Mr Dignity's second tenure.

Anyway, if Celtic's subsequent titles were going to be tainted without Rangers that would mean that if Neo-Gers were to win the Ramsden Cup that would be tainted, since Celtic wasn't in the competition. It would also mean that whoever won the Champions League or the Europa League then their wins would also be tainted since Rangers or Neo-Gers weren't taking part.

But that was missing the point, so the argument went. Celtic had no effective competition anymore in the SPL so it was essentially a one-horse race. The same, however, could be said about Neo-Gers. What competition was there in a team of full-time, SPL players against part-time teams comprised of teachers, policemen and social workers?

Ah, but Neo-Gers can only play what's in front of them. But surely the same could be said for Celtic? That's when things became surreal. Apparently it wasn't the fault of Neo-Gers that they were in the position they were in; it was all down to Peter Lawwell threatening the other clubs to throw 'Rangers' into the lower leagues so that Celtic could win title after title. Effectively, 'Rangers' had been the victims of cheating!

Incredible as it may seem, The People honestly seemed to believe this. Especially in light of the First Tier Tax Tribunal findings it was clear to them that Rangers had done nothing wrong. The club was punished for Craig Whyte's sins and 'relegated' out of sheer bigotry, vindictiveness and self-interest. This was the story that Jabba put about and The People clung to it desperately.

Celtic were 'running scared' of Neo-Gers and that was why Peter Lawwell had them thrown into the bottom tier. Some of The People went even further, suggesting that the whole tax case had been part of a Lawwell-inspired conspiracy to remove Rangers from the equation and leave the way open to title win after title win; maybe even surpassing Rangers' glorious record. The possibility of Celtic doing this haunted all the nightmares of The People.

Meanwhile, Sooperally's team showed that it was just as well that they were in the bottom tier. They struggled even against the part-timers and were soundly thrashed when they came up against full-time opponents. Queen of the South knocked them out of the Ramsden Cup in a penalty shoot-out, Terry Butcher's Inverness thrashed them 3-0 in the League Cup and Dundee United won by the same margin in the Scottish Cup. So what competition would Neo-Gers have offered in the SPL? Obviously it made no difference whether they were there or not; Celtic would still have won it comfortably.

The only bright spot for Sooperally was when his team beat Motherwell 2-0 in the League Cup. Mind you, Motherwell haven't managed to beat an Ibrox team since December 2002; a quite deplorable, and some would say suspicious, record. In fact, the only teams in the current top tier (2013-2014) that have worse records are Ross County, Hamilton and Partick Thistle. These three teams, however, have hardly been in the top tier for any length of time. What's Motherwell's excuse?

While Sooperally's team huffed and puffed, making heavy weather against supposedly far inferior opposition, their cheerleaders in the media were ready with the excuses. Mark Hateley led the way here, blaming those that had walked away from Green's new club. Since he, and all the rest, was peddling the story that it was the 'same club' then it was obvious that he would argue that TUPE regulations should have applied.

Green, believing all the hype, his own and everyone else's, decided to sue the players that had left for breach of contract. This, of course, begs the question of whom their contracts were with. It couldn't possibly have been the club, since the club was not a trading entity; the contracts must have been with the holding company. If Green was arguing that the contracts were with the club, which he claims to have bought, then the club must have been doing business on its own without any holding company involved. If that was the case, then this 'same club' should be stumping up the money owed to all those creditors.

In answer to this sheer brass neck, the Professional Football Association decided to sue Green, on behalf of the ex-Rangers players, for constructive dismissal. As with any counter-suit, the aim was not to win money but to get the pursuer of the original claim to see sense and back off. Sense and Ibrox, however, have been strangers for a long, long time.

And so Mark Hateley decided to go all-out with a character assassination on Kyle Lafferty for his unforgivable treachery. He said, in his Daily Record column,

> Lafferty has shown himself to be a selfish man and a stupid one. God knows, he wasn't even a good Rangers player. He certainly didn't come remotely close to providing value for the money – more than £3million – he cost them before heading to Swiss side Sion. He was a self-centred liability then and remains so today.[3]

Oo-er, missus; he didn't hold back, did he? Of course, in the summer of 2011 this is what Hateley was saying about Lafferty, 'He never stops working for the team — even if sometimes he works too hard. His enthusiasm is great, and if he channels that enthusiasm into the right areas, I think you will see the best of Kyle.' He also praised Lafferty for the amazing contribution he had made to Rangers at the end of the 2010-11 season.[4] What a difference a year makes!

Since Rangers had been cheated by HMRC, the football authorities and even its own players, it was only natural that The People started to demand the prize money that Rangers had 'won' by coming second in the SPL last season. Yes, they were that delusional!

The Big Lie stated categorically that Craig Whyte had cheated not only the tax man but Rangers as well. Considering he didn't seem to walk away with a load of cash, it's hard to see how he cheated Rangers. On the contrary, it was every other team in the SPL that he cheated, as he withheld the PAYE money to keep a team on the pitch. Since he, and by extension Rangers, cheated his way through the season, every game played by Rangers should have been amended to a 3-0 defeat (even the games against Motherwell). So, effectively, they should have finished last in the league and won bugger all!

This attitude of being cheated grew into a firm belief that 'Rangers' had been the recipient of undue and excessive punishments. The points deduction had allowed Celtic to win the 2011-12 SPL title, Rangers had been 'relegated' to Division 3, they had to suffer a transfer embargo and they were not allowed into Europe for three years.

Of course, these 'punishments' were nothing of the sort. The points deduction was automatic for going into administration but Celtic won the league by more points than the deduction would have made up, a whole twenty, to be precise. 'Rangers' had not been relegated; it was a new team and had been allowed into the leagues. As to not being allowed into Europe, that was down to UEFA being far more law-abiding than our own football authorities. Three years' audited accounts were required to take part in European competitions. The same was true of Scottish competitions, but that didn't stop our authorities riding roughshod over the rules!

All of this, however, fell on deaf ears. As far as The People were concerned, they had been cheated and hard-done-by. Their friends in the media, meanwhile, did all they could to try to justify this paranoia. Here's what Jabba had to say, 'What was the point and what were the real motives behind the zeal with which some in HMRC, and the media, tackled this case?' He goes on, 'Blind hatred and poison has saturated this case' and 'It's clear now who the guilty parties are and Rangers are not among them.'

Jabba also called for the identities of the tax inspectors to be revealed. He said, 'But the Revenue didn't want the names of any of their people out in there in the public domain. Why? Because we'd then know who had rejected the £10m? Or was it felt they had to be protected for other reasons?'[5]

21

This was being completely disingenuous. Jabba knew full well why the identities of these folk had to be protected; if revealed there was every chance that they, and their families, would be targeted by The People. We had already seen the violent extremes to which these maniacs could go. Not that that would worry Jabba in the slightest.

HMRC were only doing what they are supposed to do; go after tax dodgers. That is part of the law of the land. To Jabba, however, the law of the land meant nothing; only Rangers mattered. His attitude led to speculation among the Internet Bampots: was Jabba angling for a job with the new Ibrox regime?

4
Career Opportunities

As the first half of the season wore on it was obvious to all that Jabba was losing the plot. Even his pal, David Leggat, on his bigoted blog full of spelling mistakes, grammatical errors and the overuse of hyperbole, didn't go as far as Jabba did in manically lashing out at everyone. Nobody was safe. Reading his columns during the months from September to November, he outlined a sinister conspiracy, involving internet bloggers, HMRC, the SFA, the SPL, all Scotland's football clubs and supporters, Scottish journalists in the press, radio and television and, most especially, Craig Whyte to destroy Rangers. This campaign had been carefully orchestrated and carried out with ruthless efficiency. It was only by the Grace of God and Charles Green that there was a team left playing at Ibrox at all.

Of course, there was nothing new in Jabba being a mouthpiece for Ibrox; even Chick Young had accused him of such during their infamous, on-air argument. He had been a fawning cheerleader for David Murray for years and, even now, could not admit that Murray had done anything untoward. In fact, most of the pieces written about Rangers in the Daily Record during Murray's reign seemed to just be press releases from Murray's PR. Nothing was ever questioned or looked at too closely. Not surprisingly, Jabba was sports editor at the Record during much of this time. His partiality oozed through all the back pages.

A glaring example was when Walter Smith said that the football authorities in Scotland should be pulling out all the stops to help Rangers in their quest for the UEFA Cup in 2008. Jabba agreed wholeheartedly with this, saying that other countries did this, reorganizing games etc to help their representatives in European competitions. Why shouldn't the same thing happen in Scotland?

Walter Smith and Rangers, although claiming that they didn't ask for an extension to SPL fixtures, were livid in their condemnation of the extension when it came: it wasn't long enough! The Scottish Cup final was also postponed to help Rangers out in Europe, without asking the other finalists, Queen of The South.

Jabba agreed, implicitly and explicitly with these decisions. If Rangers were to win their semi-final match, then 'The SPL would have to allow them a free week in which to prepare and inevitably that would mean extending the campaign. 'If that happens there should be no argument, no moaning and no accusations of bias. It would be simple, straightforward commonsense.'[1]

Wind the clock back five years to 2003 and Celtic was in the same position. Instead of demanding extensions, though, Celtic brought games forward, with the cooperation of the opposing teams. Martin O'Neill was, however, annoyed with the prospect of having to play Rangers less than seventy-two hours after a UEFA Cup semi-final. The fixture could easily have been moved but both Rangers and the SPL point-blank refused. And Jabba's reaction?

'Just what the hell were you playing at Celtic?' he fumed. And 'Someone really ought to tell Ian McLeod and Martin O'Neill to keep their mouths shut, at least until they actually know what they're talking about.'[2] There's nothing like being consistent, eh?

He always liked to go on about the paranoia of Celtic supporters, especially when it came to arguments about Rangers getting favours from match officials. He contended that these things 'evened themselves out over the season'. Officials made mistakes in all games and there was no single team that benefited from them more than any other.

This attitude changed completely when the new season got underway in August 2008. Still hurting from Rangers getting trounced in the UEFA Cup final, The People attempting to destroy Manchester and Celtic winning the league title, the agnivores were looking for the least thing that they could moan about. They soon found it. Celtic got a few decisions going their way, including penalty kicks, which were, shall we say, a bit lucky. Strangely, there was none of the 'these things even themselves out' over this season. Our media was absolutely blazing.

Chick Young blasted out his anger and frustration on the BBC Website. He said, 'Another week, another questionable refereeing decision, another dodgy penalty.' He also came out with, '…who needs international players when match officials are doing the business for you?' Without a trace of irony, he went on in the same piece about Celtic fans being paranoid![3]

The Daily Record ran a number of stories about these 'dodgy decisions' and called it 'Refsgate'.[4] They created such a stink that a meeting had to be called at Hampden to assure SPL managers that there would be no more 'mistakes'. This had never happened before so why was it so necessary in 2008? Why didn't they just come out with the old line about 'honest mistakes'?

As it came closer to the first Old Firm derby of the season, on August 31st, the Daily Record paid more and more attention to the referee that would be officiating, one Dougie McDonald. (Yes, him.) He was interviewed in the paper to see if he was up to the job. The piece said, 'Match officials have never been under more scrutiny following a series of high-profile controversies involving the SPL's big two.' These controversies were that 'St Mirren were left furious with ref Eddie Smith over his decision to award Celtic a penalty and send off defender Will Haining at Parkhead on the opening weekend of the season. Dundee United were denied a penalty a week later after Gary Caldwell clearly tripped Roy O'Donovan inside the box,' and 'Walter Smith was left raging when DaMarcus Beasley had a last-minute winner at Pittodrie wrongly disallowed for offside.'[5] Well, we couldn't have that, could we?

Big Yogi Hughes, Falkirk manager at the time, was also wheeled out to complain about a referee at Celtic Park, under the screaming headline: 'REFSGATE THE SAGA CONTINUES'.[6] Of course, such a name for all these errors, Refsgate, implied that they weren't errors at all but part of some great conspiracy.

The tin hat was put on the whole thing when the Daily Record hired a psychiatrist to give his opinion of Dougie McDonald. Fortunately, he was proven sane, which, in Daily Record-speak, meant that he kicked with the right foot.

Fast forward a couple of years and things were back to normal. Rangers were getting dodgy decisions going their way and when Celtic fans complained they were called paranoid and the old excuse of things evening out over the season was trotted out. I telephoned Jabba's Radio Scotland show to ask why there was no Refsgate this season.

Jabba and his female assistant professed never to have heard of

Refsgate and asked me to tell them about it. I related some of the stuff above, about which Jabba seemed to have no recollection at all. Surely he remembered engaging a psychiatrist, I asked, since that was such an unusual occurrence. His reply was that he had merely, as sports editor, signed the cheques and didn't look too closely into what they were for!

I said that the evidence would be there in the Daily Record archives and perhaps he could have a look the next time he was in his office. He promised that he would and if he found that they had hired a psychiatrist he would contact him and send him round to me!

Before I could say, 'Ya cheeky fat bastard!' I was summarily cut off.

This was Jabba's usual way of dealing with people that presented him with an awkward truth; tell them that they were paranoid or suffering from some mental illness. Hopefully he did get the name and number of that psychiatrist because the way his articles were going in 2012 Jabba himself would be requiring the doctor's services.

Jabba was also a great believer in a Darwinian, Survival of the Fittest, theory of football. He was always banging on about how football was a business first and foremost. Even when the team he supported, (no sniggering at the back, there) Airdrie, went to the wall he was not too concerned. That was life in the economic jungle; red in tooth and claw. The fact that it was David Murray that put Airdrie out of business probably swayed how Jabba felt.

He used the same kind of argument for his contention that Neo-Gers should have been welcomed straight into the SPL. Sporting integrity, the rules or any other considerations could all go to hell; what mattered was that money would be lost if there was no Rangers, or its equivalent, in the top tier. His favourite expression was, 'Scottish football will survive without Rangers but it won't thrive without Rangers.'

All of which makes clear his hypocrisy when he was suddenly beating the drum for the lower leagues. In September 2012 he had this to say about the SFL, '…their league is a better example of a collective and they connect in more profound ways with their communities as well as the Scottish Government, who have enormous respect for what the SFL are doing in difficult times.' He also contended that, 'It wouldn't surprise me if the SFL do come up with a new and radical structure that addresses a whole range of issues.'[7]

A complete change of heart then; now it was SPL bad, SFL good. No more devil-take-the-hindmost, market forces for our Jabba. Now everything was all about the good of the game. And if anyone believed that then they were as crazy as Jabba was acting.

With the end of the year fast approaching, Jabba and his colleagues were disappointed to see that the prophesied Armageddon showed no signs of happening yet. Celtic managed to beat Barcelona 2-1 at Celtic Park, which went against all the doom and gloom coming from Jabba's poison pen. There were plaudits galore for Celtic's achievement, except, of course, from The People, who argued that Barcelona were a weaker team than they used to be. Jabba just ignored the match completely!

What he decided to concentrate on was the 'crisis' at Hearts. This, apparently, was all down to Green's Neo-Gers being denied entry to the SPL.[8] Seemingly we were back to economic forces now instead of the good of the game. I don't think I can ever remember a time when there wasn't a 'crisis' at Hearts. Remember Wallace Mercer's attempt at amalgamation with Hibs? For years it seemed as if Hearts were going to go to the wall; but they were still here. It was hardly the best example for Jabba to use to bolster his argument!

As the weeks went by Jabba became more and more unhinged. He said of everyone outside of Ibrox that it 'suits their agenda to link all debts run up by the previous regime to the club in the Third Division. Yet the same folk are determined to make sure Rangers aren't linked with all of the league titles won in the past.'[9]

Strangely he couldn't see the corollary of this. It suited Jabba, his fellow journalists and those in power at Ibrox to link Neo-Gers with all the league titles won by the old Rangers. When it came to the debts, however, it was a different matter entirely. So which group was in the wrong: those that say either pay up or admit you're a new club, or those that stick two fingers up to all the creditors but still want to claim the old honours? I think that's an easy one for anyone with any decency.

By the end of November Jabba's hypocrisy knew no bounds. He was desperately trying to undermine the SPL in any way he could. Stephen Thompson, the chairman of Dundee United, resigning from the SPL Board was an opportunity he couldn't pass up. The story was that Thompson resigned due to 'professional differences,' a phrase that usually means that there was a falling-out somewhere along the line. Jabba, however, decided on a different tack.

He said that Thompson 'stood accused' of 'drip-feeding' stories to the media.[10] He gave no examples of any of these stories, who they were 'drip-fed' to or how damaging they were. In fact, nobody else had this story about Thompson; it was a Jabba 'exclusive'. So how did Jabba find out about this? From 'SPL sources,' of course! So Jabba was drip-fed a story about somebody drip-feeding stories. And he wondered why hardly anybody took him seriously anymore?

And then, finally, at the beginning of December, Jabba decided to say farewell to the world of journalism. Of course, he couldn't go quietly. In his final column in the Daily Record he said he had 'happy memories'; sadly, he did not recount too many of those. Most of his column was taken up with a bile-laden condemnation of just about everybody.

> Even now so many – and I include some fellow journalists – still cannot bring themselves to accept Rangers did not cheat the tax man by using EBTs.
> Just when did they become consumed by such eye-popping rage? Was it always there, a dormant fury against Rangers and their fans…?
> Despicable, pathetic little creatures craving some kind of recognition but lacking in conscience and morality.
> However, that's it. My work here is done and I'm glad – but just for the record, I've not been sacked or made redundant. I was asked to remain but my conscience won't allow me to stay in our profession. The kind of journalism needed by the country, never mind sport, no longer exists in enough of the media outlets.[11]

So that was it. He was walking off in the huff because everybody didn't share his slavish devotion to Rangers and Neo-Gers. In his eyes every media outlet in the land should be spouting Charles Green's PR propaganda. The fact that the media had gone along with the Big Lie that it was the 'same club' didn't matter one bit; they weren't doing enough.

So had that loose screw finally fallen out or had Jabba been indulging, as some Internet Bampots claimed, in the longest job application in history? As it turned out, the latter was the case. It came as no surprise to anyone when it was announced that Jabba was going to be employed at Ibrox.

What was a surprise was his new title, Director of Communications. After slandering practically all the sports journalists in Scotland he was hardly going to be a great PR man, was he? And what about new communications platforms? Could Jabba lower himself to actually use the internet, like all those 'despicable, pathetic little creatures'? He was hardly an expert in communications in any case. I have already said how he treated callers to his radio programme that he didn't agree with. Great communications skills there, eh?

As for the 'Director' bit; from Jabba's recent utterances, it would be hard to find anyone that would trust him to be able to direct his pish into a bucket.

So how long had Jabba been angling for a job at Ibrox? As it turned out, he had been touting himself well before Green appeared. In 2013 texts appeared that had been sent between Jabba and Craig Whyte a whole year and more previously. These were exposed online, along with a lot of other texts, e-mails and recorded phone calls, by somebody calling themselves Charlotte Fakes.

The newspapers were too scared to print any of this stuff, especially after the Leveson Inquiry. Bloggers were made of sterner stuff. Even Neo-Gers supporters' blogs were not averse to using some of the things revealed by Charlotte Fakes whenever it suited their agenda. The fact that nobody came out and denied any of Charlotte Fakes's revelations led many to assume that they were the truth.

Anyway, one of the series of texts between Jabba and Whyte was about an article Jabba was writing for the Sunday Mail back in July 2011. Amazingly, or, then again, maybe predictably, he sent the article to Whyte for his approval before publishing it. Whyte suggested an alteration and the article duly appeared, minus the bit that Whyte had objected to.

The second lot of texts was much more damning. They were sent back and forth on January 6th 2012. The date is significant.

> Hi Craig, haven't been sacked, haven't resigned despite all the rumours. However, I'm almost certain I can get out within weeks if I insist. Do you want to talk? JT
> Hi Jim, I'm back in Glasgow next Friday. Let's meet up then and discuss. C

> Okay, see you then.[12]

This was at a time when we were told that Jabba was 'sitting' on a major story concerning Rangers. The story was finally broken in the Daily Record on 31st January. It was the big revelation that Whyte had made a deal with Ticketus to pay off the debt to Lloyds Bank.[13] It makes you wonder why he was 'sitting' on this story, eh?

The most damning indictment of Jabba came after he left, when Keith Jackson wrote an encomium in the Daily Record. Instead of telling us what a great man Jabba was, Jackson could only lambast everyone that 'drove him out' of journalism. In fact, he could only find two 'good' things to say about Jabba; he was 'Machiavellian' and 'brutal'.[14] It would hardly make a great epitaph, would it?

5
Hate and War

Given the insistence of Jabba, and just about everybody else in our media, that Rangers, i.e. Green's Neo-Gers, had been cheated and ill-used by the whole of Scottish football, it was only natural that the thoughts of The People would turn to vengeance. Chris Graham set the ball rolling, with his 'Enemies of Glasgow Rangers' list. The idea was that note should be made of every anti-Rangers utterance or action and when 'Rangers' were 'back' to their 'rightful place' at the top of Scottish football, 'Zen ve shall examine Ze List!'

The pettiness of The People was shown clearly on this pathetic website. Along with the expected suspects, like Peter Lawwell and Neil Lennon he had some more obscure names, like the Vespbar, which, as you might guess is a bar. So what did he have against this establishment? Well, he spouts a load of pish about deleted tweets but his main evidence is this tweet, sent to Celtic fans: 'Got the Celtic game on today, showing on our big screen (120 inches). Ice cream and jelly at full time.'[1] That's his criterion for hatred and possible incitement to violence. Either that or the idea of all those inches brought out some deep-seated inferiority complex.

Graham's blog disappeared as soon as he started to play Mr Respectable Fan's Representative in the press and on the telly. Some civic-minded souls, however, preserved copies, which are easily found on the internet. Others, however, were ready to pick up where Graham left off. David Leggat, the blogger-that-used-to-be-a-journalist, was one such individual.

And when Rangers and Rangers supporters are back on top once more and looking down again on Dundee United, on Hearts, on Hibs, on St Mirren on Motherwell and on all theothers who have behaved in such a horrible twisted, warped and bigoted way, let Rangers and let Rangers supporters take a terrible revenge on them.[2]

Thus spake Leggat, leaving hardly any of the country unthreatened. No doubt there were folk the length and breadth of Scotland shitting themselves that festive season. How to make friends and influence people, eh?

I don't know what form this revenge was going to take but it wouldn't be too hard to guess. The bombs sent to Neil Lennon and others were one clue, as was the destruction in Manchester in 2008. Then we had the death threats to Phil Mac Giolla Bhain, the Scottish Sun and even the BBC when it dared show the extent of the EBT scheme.

Imagine if Leggat's threats were made on some Islamic website; what do you think would have happened? His feet wouldn't have touched the ground as he was whisked away to that special jail near Govan where they keep terrorists. Writing a hate speech and incitement to violence would be the least of the charges thrown at him. But when it's one of The People it seems there's no law against writing anything.

The chosen candidates for 'Ze List' began to get ridiculous. The Daily Record (who else?) howled in indignant moral outrage at a banner displayed by the Green Brigade at Celtic Park.[3] It showed the de-evolution from Homo Sapiens, to Homo Erectus to Rangers-scarf-wearing ape. The next stage in this backwards evolution was a grave, marking where Rangers had died. Then we had a zombie with a Rangers scarf coming out of the grave. It was a hilarious parody. Unfortunately, whoever made the thing didn't think it through. The normal way to dispose of a zombie is to shoot it in the head, so the banner had a gunman getting rid of the Rangers zombie.

Of course, this left the door open for The People to claim that the banner was 'terrorist-inspired'. Leggat was all over this, claiming that the banner was about the IRA![4] The Daily Record helped things along by lying that the gunman had a shamrock on his sleeve.[5] The whole point of the banner was lost in this nonsense.

All these claims about the banner being 'terrorist-inspired' were, however, nothing more than a rationalisation. I think it was Jim Delahunt on Radio Clyde that said that the banner was actually pretty funny up to the point where the gunman appeared. The resultant angry phone calls, e-mails, letters and death threats to Radio Clyde showed that the ire over the banner had nothing whatsoever to do with the gunman.

BBC Scotland found itself on Ze List, again, for an opening sequence on Sportscene. It was a kind of cartoon, based on the opening credits for the programme 'Mad Men' and showed Sooperally falling helplessly towards the ground. The original sequence in 'Mad Men' was all about how the main character was being buffeted about by all kinds of influences beyond his control. In that respect it was a pretty sympathetic portrayal of Sooperally, who seemed to be struggling to hold things together while things were falling apart all around him. The People, of course, saw things differently.

As with the Green Brigade banner, The People groped around to find something to be offended over. They latched onto the two girls that had jumped from the Kingston Bridge, even though that incident had happened three years previously. They condemned the 'crass insensitivity' of the BBC for showing this on 'the anniversary' of the tragic deaths of those troubled teenagers. You get the impression, however, that The People would have grasped at anything to be outraged about.

Consequently, another name was added to Ze List; that of Tam Cowan. Cowan is classed as a comedian but is hardly in the Frankie Boyle league, both in terms of being funny and of being offensive. He is the kind of comedian that makes you groan rather than laugh; in other words, he is pretty harmless. He is also not what you would call partisan; he pokes fun at everybody, Celtic, Rangers, Neo--Gers and even his beloved Motherwell. Unlike other folk that write about football in Scotland, Cowan supports who he says he supports; you will actually find him at Fir Park wearing a Motherwell scarf. So what did he do to earn the ire of The People?

You won't believe this but all he did was say that the Sportscene 'Mad Men' spoof was quite funny. This was enough to get Leggat's Presbyterian granny's knickers in a twist. In fact, Cowan denied even saying it at all. Which one of those two would you believe? Others joined in the hate-fest, maintaining that Cowan had always had it in for Rangers, while being soft on Celtic. Cowan never mentioned whether or not he received any death threats, but I wouldn't be at all surprised.

To Cowan's credit, he refused to be bullied and even poked fun at

33

Leggat and his Presbyterian granny.[6] Surprisingly, he wasn't sacked by the Daily Record, although I'm guessing he was *persona non grata* in the sports department, especially since he seemed to enjoy pointing out that they were all bluenoses!

It wasn't all death threats, however; some saner minds suggested a different kind of revenge. This vengeance was a financial one; when they 'got back' to the top tier The People would boycott all away matches. That would teach all 'those reptiles from the Scottish Premier League,' as Leggat called them.[7]

Strangely, nobody bothered to think this one through to its logical conclusion. If none of the other clubs were going to benefit from Neo-Gers being in the SPL then it made no difference if they were there or not. All we had heard about in our media was how Armageddon was coming; without The People to spend their money at away matches then all the SPL clubs would struggle to break even. Now they were saying that if they were in the SPL they would refuse to attend away matches anyway. The message this sent was loud and clear: who the hell needed them?

It appeared that The People had learnt nothing. It was hubris that had led to the death of their old club, while they all stood around shouting, 'We are The People,' and did nothing to help. Even when they raised money it was called 'The Rangers Fans Fighting Fund' and was not intended to help out the club but to fight their imagined enemies. That was all they could think of, fighting; not to save their club but against everybody else.

When the CVA proposal, which only amounted to about 8 pence in the pound and would reduce to a fraction of a penny to the pound if the First Tier Tax Tribunal went in HMRC's favour, was rejected Green was pointing the finger of blame again. He said,

> I can understand HMRC deciding that football clubs which do not pay their taxes need to be punished, but by effectively banning Rangers from Europe for three years all that will happen is that there will be less revenue generated by the club and consequently less money paid over to the taxman.[8]

Not one word of apology was ever forthcoming from Ibrox about all the creditors that had been swindled. Instead, following Green's lead, they were blaming everybody else, including HMRC. All the creditors could go and fuck themselves; who were they next to the 'Famous Glasgow Rangers'? The only surprising thing was that none of the creditors received death threats! After all, The People wanted revenge on everybody.

They had an opportunity of taking some of this threatened vengeance when they were due to meet Dundee United at Tannadice in the Scottish Cup in February. There were numerous calls for a boycott, leading to Green actually refusing to accept his club's allocation of tickets. He said, 'Everyone at this club is dismayed at the actions of certain SPL clubs, which were actively engaged in trying to harm Rangers.'[9] This was an astute political move on Green's part. Any lingering doubts about him would hopefully now be dispelled; he was trying to prove himself to be one of The People.

And so the Big Lie got bigger as it went on, as lies tend to do. Not only was Green's Neo-Gers touted as still being Rangers, but that had expanded to make everything a big conspiracy. Since Green's club was not a new one but the same, old Rangers then they should automatically have been in the SPL. In that case the SPL clubs acted illegally in 'demoting' Green's club to the lower leagues. Such illegal and immoral acts demanded vengeance!

No matter what The People decided to believe in place of reality, one fact could not be disputed; Neo-Gers wouldn't have managed to stay in the SPL. They'd obviously be guaranteed twelve points against Motherwell but, otherwise, they'd be taken apart game after game. Why the hell would anybody want that?

Still, there's no reasoning with some people, especially The People. In their eyes they were still the all-conquering team of the 1990s and would win any league they were placed in. So they were willing to accept the 'stab in the back' story; just like right-wingers did in Germany after the First World War and in America after the Vietnam War. Where would it all lead? We'd have to wait and see.

6
Guns on the Roof

After his scare when the attempt was made to get rid of him as soon as he'd got the keys to Ibrox, Charles Green was obviously desperate to suck up to The People. November gave him a major opportunity. Over the previous couple of years, they had gone overboard at Ibrox when it came to Remembrance Day. Green decided he was going to outdo them all and get all the Unionist flag-wavers on his side.

During the last number of years there has been a radical shift in how Remembrance Day is viewed in Britain. I remember when I was at primary school we would have a minute's silence (two minutes is too long for a lot of children!). Our headmaster had been in the RAF and was insistent on observing the silence. I don't know about other schools but, from what I've heard, the same thing happened.

When I was eight I was in the Boys' Brigade and we would have a solemn parade at the local Church of Scotland on Remembrance Sunday. We moved house and when I was ten I joined the Scouts. Again I attended solemn parades on Remembrance Sunday, this time at the Catholic Church.

These ceremonies still go on and the silence is still observed in schools but there has been a change in the perception of what the whole thing is about. Instead of thinking about, and praying for, those that died in the wars, it has become all about support for the armed forces. Now it is all about Jingoism, flag waving and even hatred. In short, the whole thing has been hijacked by people as bad as those our predecessors fought against in the Second World War.

It wasn't just what Remembrance Day stood for that changed; now you were expected to wear a poppy during the weeks leading up to 11th November. If you didn't wear one, then you were castigated for being disrespectful. Jon Snow, the Channel 4 News presenter, found himself on the receiving end of this 'Poppy Fascism' when he maintained his right to only wear his poppy on the day itself.[1] By 2012 author Dr Ted Harrison was bemoaning the commercialism of the whole thing, citing the availability of poppy golf umbrellas and jewellery, which folk could carry and wear all year round to show their patriotism.[2]

And patriotism seemed to be what it was all about now. It was getting so that people were scared not to wear a poppy. Watch the BBC during November and everybody's wearing one, probably whether they want to or not. Even some foreigner, invited on to discuss the situation in Egypt or whatever has a poppy slapped on his jacket, while he sits there thinking it's some strange, British custom.

And then you get the lunatics that write into the papers and post on their forums, suggesting that everybody refuses to use a shop if the folk there aren't wearing poppies, while shopkeepers should refuse to serve anyone not wearing one. It's getting like the 'mark of the Beast' in the Book of Revelation!

Anyone that thinks the poppy is still sacrosanct and is just about remembering the war dead should look at Lieutenant General Sir John Kiszely. Who? Well, this guy was President of the Royal British Legion. He had to resign in October 2012 after being caught in a Sunday Times sting operation. He had bragged to the undercover reporters, who were pretending to represent a South Korean arms company, that he could easily lobby the Defence Secretary on their behalf. He said 'his role at the legion gave him access to important figures in defence, and described the annual remembrance events as a 'tremendous networking opportunity.'[3] It just shows how low Remembrance Day and the poppy charity had sunk.

Football became affected by all this nonsense as well. It was no longer enough to have a minute's, or two minutes', silence at the start of a match; now the players had to wear special shirts with poppies on them. If a team, or an individual player, played without poppies on display then all the screeching and finger-pointing started.

James McClean refused to wear the shirt with the poppy on it when he played for Sunderland in 2012. He was a Republic of Ireland international, who had grown up in Derry as part of the Nationalist community and obviously had no great love for the British armed forces. Of course, McClean was roundly condemned for showing disrespect and for bringing politics into the remembrance of our war dead.

His Sunderland teammate, Connor Wickham, whose father was in the army, posted the following on Twitter: 'Support for the troops past and present before game today is great! We should be proud of our troops!'[4] This statement showed how much things had changed and the poppy was no longer a symbol of those that had died in two world wars but was all about support for the armed forces and for current wars.

A lot of folk can't seem to be able to distinguish between respect for war dead and support for armed forces, but there is a world of difference. Irish people, and those of Irish descent, have no problem remembering and respecting those that died in the wars; after all, many Irishmen lost their lives in these conflicts as well. The problem for these folk wasn't the ones that died; it was the ones that came back from the trenches.

After the First World War many ex-servicemen were sent to Ireland to augment the police force there. They were known as the Black and Tans and they became notorious for their widespread use of torture and murder, usually for no other reason than sheer prejudice. My own great-great-grandmother had petrol poured over her and was set alight, while the Black and Tans laughed and took bets on how long it would take her to die. Anybody that tried to intervene was subjected to a beating.

Atrocities like this were commonplace and most Irish families have similar, or worse, stories to tell. To me it's in the distant past but to those that still have a connection to Northern Ireland it's aggravated by the rawness still felt due to Bloody Sunday and revelations about the British army colluding with Unionist terrorists during the Troubles.

And it's not just those with an Irish connection that feel uneasy about supporting our armed forces. Such support tends to go hand-in-hand with support for the wars they are currently engaged in. Many people in this country are completely against our being involved in the Middle East, feeling that we're just being dragged into America's wars. Stories of atrocities committed by our troops hardly help matters.

In this light it's understandable that some folk don't want to wear poppies to 'support our armed forces' and the demonstrations against the poppies at Celtic Park make a lot more sense. If it was still just about remembering the war dead, then such demonstrations wouldn't take place at all.

And so we come to The People, who still seem to live in a time when Britannia ruled the waves. In their minds our armed forces can do no wrong and if they commit atrocities, well they must have been provoked into it. The same goes for war; there is no such thing as an unjust war if Britain is involved and the only thing that matters is that British forces emerge triumphant.

To give you an example, one contributor to McMurdo's website posted Wilfred Owen's poem, 'Dulce et decorum est'. We've all had to study this poem at school so everybody knows how Owen felt about the war and what he was saying about it. He even calls the phrase 'dulce et decorum est pro patria mori' a 'lie'. Incredibly, the poster on McMurdo's site honestly thought that Owen was saying that it was a sweet and glorious thing to die for your country.[5] Talk about delusional!

McMurdo himself also makes the point about 'support for the troops'. He says, 'It is...a shame that the serving members of Her Majesty's Armed Forces who are Celtic supporters are not celebrated by club and fans.'[6] McMurdo is being totally disingenuous here and knows full well what the problem is with many Celtic supporters; in fact, he's pointed it out himself with his 'Armed Forces...celebrated' bit. That's not what Remembrance Day is supposed to be about.

This was the zeitgeist in which Charles Green was operating and so he decided to go the whole hog and turn Remembrance Day into a three-ring circus. Marines abseiling from the roof, armed forces marching behind a pipe band at half-time, then wandering around getting pictures taken with players and having a wee kick-about and artillery guns firing, all combined to make it a show that PT Barnum would have been proud of. Instead of Remembrance Day it was billed as Armed Forces Day, just to make sure that nobody was in any doubt what the purpose of this fol-de-rols was.

Of course, not everyone was impressed by this display. The sight of armed forces personnel smiling and laughing and kicking footballs about was hardly in keeping with what was supposed to be a solemn ceremony of remembrance. Complaints were sent to the top brass in the armed forces and they agreed that the scenes at Ibrox were inappropriate.

A letter to one complainant outlined that the Scottish military top brass felt that:

> ...the format of the half-time event and the conduct of those

39

taking part in it was inappropriate for Remembrance weekend and will take steps to ensure that such events are conducted with appropriate solemnity in the future.

They believe that the minute's silence before the match was the correct way to mark the occasion and Army commanders will be directed to restrict future Remembrance events to this type of activity in the future.[7]

There was one interesting item raised by the Army Secretariat in the letter. It was pointed out that 'The focus of Remembrance activities must be on the fallen, not on those who are serving in the Armed Forces today.'[8] That sentence should be given wider circulation so that we can get back to what Remembrance Day is supposed to be about, instead of the current right-wing jingo-fest.

An Ibrox spokesman told the Daily Record, 'the club have a close relationship with the services and will continue to mark Remembrance Day with proper respect.'[9] A close relationship with the services? I don't remember Rangers indulging in these antics until fairly recently. Even the Daily Record, although saying 'The club have regularly honoured the Armed Forces on match days over the years,'[10] could only go as far back as 2009 to provide any kind of example. This was around the time that the poppy was changing from being a symbol of remembrance to a symbol of support. Rangers and Neo-Gers were just falling into line with the general political climate in Britain.

Of course, The People were none-too-pleased about their display of support being banned. 'Now we cannot even support our troops in Scotland!' one blog bleated.[11] This missed the entire point, probably disingenuously. Nobody was stopping anyone from supporting whomever they liked; all that was being asked was that they didn't hijack Remembrance Day to do it! The club itself reacted in a more level-headed way and decided, in future, to have a separate Armed Forces Day.

The reaction of The People in general was that the armed forces hierarchy had acquiesced to a bigoted minority. One character wrote a letter of epic proportions to the Defence Secretary, among others, to vent his outrage. He likened the event to funeral parades in New Orleans and even to Catholic funeral services! He attempted to maintain a cultured, intellectual vein to his letter but fell down by, like others, quoting Wifred Owen out of context. This lack of understanding permeated his whole epistle and, rather tragically, showed that he was missing the point entirely.[12]

Still, it was a good, political move by Charles Green. Again he had summoned the backs-to-the-wall paranoia that made The People feel that everyone was against them. Surely he had proven his credentials as a 'Real Rangers Man'?

7
Cheapskates

If anything was going to make Green's hold on the assets, and on the imaginations of The People, more permanent it was the issuing of new shares. Flotation on the stock market and the respectability of institutional investors would bring a veneer of reality to all the claims that Green's club was still Rangers. If he could get loads of money in and make it so that his team could quickly climb the leagues and overtake Celtic, then maybe he could silence all those that still hankered for 'Real Rangers Men' in charge at Ibrox.

And so the clarion call went out and the opportunity was given to The People to buy shares in their club. All of us on the outside looking in wondered if they would be so willing to part with their cash. After all, they had bought shares in their old club, only to later find out that all they had were worthless shares in a made-up holding company. Their debentures had all gone for a Burton as well. So what would they be buying into this time?

To appeal to the pockets of The People, Walter Smith was brought in as a non-executive director. 'It is a great privilege to serve the club that means so much to me,' he said as he arrived at Ibrox.[1] This was in stark contrast to what he had said a few months previously: 'We wish the new Rangers Football Club every good fortune.'[2] So somebody else had come round to the Big Lie; no doubt a healthy pay packet was great incentive.

The share issue in The Rangers International Football Club PLC was announced in the AIM alternative market in the London Stock Exchange. At least they were being honest about one thing; any shares bought actually would be shares in a holding company this time around.

It's worth looking at how this new holding-company palaver worked. The administrators, Duff and Phelps, had made an agreement with Green to sell the assets to his company, called Sevco 5088, if a CVA was not accepted. Green subsequently set up a different company, called Sevco Scotland, to buy these assets. (The reasons for this became clear several months down the line.) The actual contract of sale just said, 'Sevco,' allowing Duff and Phelps to pretend that they were selling to the same company that they had the agreement with.

The Stock Exchange was then informed that Sevco Scotland would henceforth be called, 'The Rangers Football Club PLC'. This was the new club that Green was going to tout as being 'still Rangers'. To maintain the myth that the club had been separate from the previously unheard-of holding company a discrete holding company was actually set up this time round. This was called 'The Rangers International Football Club PLC'; this was the company in which shares were being sold.

If there was, the Good Lord forbid, another liquidation in the future, then this time it would be cut-and-dried. The holding company could go bust while the club remained untouched. It was a clever move. Creating this set-up would help crystalise the myth that this is the way things had been all along.

As the share prospectus pointed out, the club had a 'loyal and passionate global fanbase' so Green had to make sure that there would be enough shares to go around. For that reason, he 'ring-fenced' £10m worth of shares for ordinary punters to buy. Hopefully that was going to be enough.

The last time there had been a share issue at Ibrox it didn't exactly set the world on fire. It was in 2004 that David Murray put £57m worth of shares up for sale. The actual figure raised was £51m, which seems successful enough until you realise that £50m of that effectively came out of Murray's pocket. His parent company, Murray International Holdings, had underwritten the share issue, and had to absorb the massive loss that had been made.

With all the debts that MIH ended up with, Lloyd's Bank had to take over much of the company and start liquidating assets. The company is still posting massive losses. Since Lloyd's Bank belongs to the tax payer then, effectively, we're all still paying for the stinginess of The People.

Surely this time would be different, though? After all, The People had to prove to everybody that their club had been saved and what better way than to actually buy shares in it. If the Big Lie was to be maintained it was essential that the share issue was a success.

Parallels were drawn with the situation at Celtic in the 1990s. Of course, Celtic never went into liquidation but, according to our media, Rangers never died either. If all went well then Green would be heralded as the Ibrox equivalent of Fergus McCann and the myth would be born of Rangers being saved from extinction by a combination of him and the fans.

The Celtic share issue had been a massive success, with ordinary fans buying £9m worth of shares. This was the equivalent of £15m in 2012. This, of course, would not be taken into account when Green's share issue brought in the expected £10m. It would be trumpeted to the heavens how Rangers supporters had invested more than the fans of Celtic.

Well before the share issue went ahead, Green claimed that they were looking to raise £20m for working capital. Now institutional investors had promised £17m his target went up to £27m, including the projected £10m from the supporters. He made lots of noises about his club being on the 'way back' and was bullish about the future.

He had good reason to feel confident; The People had all pledged online that they were going to buy so many shares that the issue would be seriously oversubscribed. Online promises are one thing, however; putting your hand in your pocket is quite another. It has to be mentioned as well that many Celtic fans took great delight in going online to pledge millions that would never materialise. Still, even half of the £22m pledged online would be more than enough.

Bill McMurdo praised the share issue, saying that Green and his fellow board members Imran Ahmad and Brian Stockbridge were 'all passionately committed to giving the fans a substantial percentage in the club's ownership. This was demonstrated when some institutional investment was refused by the club as shares were earmarked for the fans.'[3]

By 17th December it started to look as if the supporters' allocation of shares was going to be seriously undersubscribed, just like Murray's issue was. Keith Jackson did a desperate bit of last-minute rallying of the troops by pointing out that if they were to invest less than Celtic did then they would be derided by their neighbours.[4]

When the share issue closed the next day at lunchtime it soon became clear that The People had only bought about £5m worth of shares. So, despite all the bluster and swagger, The People could only muster a third of what the Celtic fans had raised! So what went wrong?

The excuses were all brought out and paraded; it was only a week before Christmas, we were in the middle of a recession etc. Leggat, of course, went his own way and blamed an 'Enemy Within' for undermining the share issue. Mind you, that didn't stop him from calling the £5m an 'astonishing' amount.[5]

In fact, this was the line taken by all of our media. Instead of the failure it was, the share issue was hailed as a triumph. Away back in October, Green had said that they hoped to raise £20m. Of course, that was the figure now used by the media, instead of the £27m broadcast at the start of the share issue, to make it appear that the whole thing had been a resounding success. Instead of being nearly £5m undersubscribed it was £2.2m over! That was mostly due to the institutional investors, of course, but that didn't stop our press going overboard. The People had rallied to the cause again.

Green said, 'I would like to thank our supporters who stepped up to the plate when asked to buy season tickets earlier in the season and have done so again at a time of year when money is extremely tight.'[6] He seemed to have forgotten that the season tickets were cheap and, even then, many of The People had managed to finagle juvenile tickets for themselves.

Sooperally said that the £5m raised was 'absolutely (does he know any other adverbs?) staggering'. He also said, rather ominously, 'I think the best way I can put it is, the one thing the investors and, certainly, the fans deserve is for their money to be used wisely.'[7] By God, that sentence was going to come back and bite him on the arse!

There were two main outcomes of the share issue. The first was that with everyone praising the contribution of the fans, including Green, it made it appear as if they had saved 'Rangers'. It was

45

their club and since they were responsible for it still being in existence they were the ones that would dictate how it was going to be run and by whom.

The second was that Green had saddled himself with a 'Rangers Man' in Walter Smith. This was a stupid move on his part. It might have seemed a good idea to bring him on board to boost the share issue and there's always the old adage about keeping your friends close but your enemies closer. That, however, is a load of bollocks and Green, as a supposedly astute businessman, should have known that. If a split was to develop in the boardroom between him and Smith, who would The People and the media support: some Johnny-come-lately or good old Mr Dignity? All Green did with this appointment was build up trouble for the future.

8
Hateful

And so 2013 arrived and it looked as if we were going to have more of the same. Keith Jackson saw out the old year with this little gem,

> Yes, 2012 will be remembered fondly by some. They will cherish the memories of how Rangers were savaged by a foaming-mouthed pack and then ripped limb from limb. These bloodthirsty ghouls would gladly watch it all happen again tomorrow, such is the depth of their hatred but it is time now for the more gentle, civilised and decent minded among us to rise up and to quietly take our ball back.[1]

I've always fancied a face-to-face with one of these hacks that peddle this garbage. I'd like to ask them what they wanted done when Rangers went into liquidation; were we all just to look the other way, pretend that Green's club was still the same Rangers and carry on as if nothing had happened? That would have set a dangerous precedent.

If Green's club had just carried on with the same licence, plying its trade in the SPL, then no team in Scotland would be extended credit ever again. The loans etc already in place would run their course but, after that it would be cash only. What bank, or any other business for that matter, would be willing to take the risk that the football club that owed them money would just go into liquidation and then carry on as normal? Scottish football would face financial ruin.

This would become a business norm in Scottish football and an easy way of keeping a club going; when things were looking bleak just liquidate and then carry on as normal. Even if clubs didn't go down this route there was always the possibility that they could. The police and ambulance services would have to be paid in advance as would anyone else needed for a match to take place. Cup games would be a nightmare as club chairmen marched up to the office as soon as the match was finished to demand their share, to be handed over in used fivers.

And what about transfers? Would foreign clubs trust Scottish teams to pay up? How many Scottish clubs could afford to stump up transfer fees up front? UEFA could hardly stand by and let Scottish football be run in such a fashion. We'd probably soon find that all our clubs were banned from European competitions while the Scotland team was banned from internationals. Is this what they wanted to happen?

But logical thought doesn't come into it where Rangers are concerned. Leggat might have banged on about seeing every non-Rangers football fan's true colours[2] but, in reality, what we saw were the true colours of our partial media and those colours were of a distinctly light-blue hue!

So even though Jabba had gone on to pastures blue, we were still being fed a pile of shit about how everybody conspired to try to kill Rangers. Funny that; when Celtic nearly went under in 1994 I don't remember any hands of friendship or help being in evidence! Sooperally had a good laugh and the Daily Record sent a hearse round to Celtic Park for a good photo opportunity. Rangers apparently sent a wreath to Celtic Park every hour. And yet, we heard nothing about 'foaming-mouthed packs' being around then.

Meanwhile Jabba made his first appearance in his new role, writing on the Neo-Gers website. And what did he have to say for himself? Nothing that he hadn't already said in the Daily Record before he stormed off in a huff. Everybody had been bad to Rangers, it was still the same team, kicking them when they were down etc etc.[3]

Of course, he was totally against the plans for league reconstruction; not that he had anything to say about the plans themselves. The only reason for his opposition was that the 'biggest club in the country' had been left out of the decision-making process.[4] No prizes for guessing which club was the 'biggest in the country'!

This was an idea that was being touted more and more on blogs and in the media; Neo-Gers was Scotland's biggest club because it looked as if they had the biggest attendance figures. Of course, these attendance figures were a combination of defiance and the cheapness of the tickets. And mere attendance figures are not the be-all-and-end-all when it comes to greatness. By that reckoning the Bay City Rollers were a much bigger group than the Sex Pistols!

Stand outside any church on a Sunday and watch the congregation coming out. Unless they happen to be filming Songs of Praise in the building that day, you'll see a small trickle of folk drifting through the door. The ministers and priests can address all the members of their congregations by name, since they see the same tiny amount of faces week in, week out. Gone are the days when you'd have six or seven masses every Sunday so as to accommodate everybody in the parish. Very few children could even tell you what Sunday School is, never mind go to it. Church attendances in every Christian denomination are at their lowest ever.

Stand outside a mosque on a Friday, however, and it's a different story. The place will be packed out. Even on other days there will be a lot of coming-and-going as different groups meet. So, since far more people attend mosque than they do church, that must mean that Islam is the country's biggest religion. Maybe we should be teaching that to our children in schools instead of Christianity!

It could be that the supporters of Rangers and then Neo-Gers have already converted to Islamic fundamentalism. After all, didn't they declare Jihad on just about everybody in Scotland in 2012?

Anyway, back to Jabba. He decided to have another go at his erstwhile fellow-journalists, warning them to be careful what they said about his new employers in future.[5] And this guy was the Director of Communications? The way he was going nobody in their right mind would ever want to communicate with him again!

And even more madness was coming out of Ibrox. Green and Sooperally were both bleating about proposals for a three-division set up under league reconstruction. They were moaning about the fact that they might still be in the 'bottom league,' in this new set up. The fact was, however, that, if they were good enough, it wouldn't take them any longer to get 'back' to the top tier. It seemed, though, that they couldn't get by without constantly playing the victim.

'We'll have to play the same teams again that we played against this season,' they whined. And what the hell do they think would have happened if they had been allowed to walk straight into the SPL? It looked as if nothing would please them unless theirs was the only team left in Scotland!

For the rest of January and into February, all we heard about was 'Rangers haters' and 'The enemies of Rangers' both on blogs and in the papers. The most deranged part of all this was that the bloggers, including Jabba on the Neo-Gers website, were constantly accusing the press of saying that Green's club was a new one. In reality, the press was doing nothing of the sort. Not one of our hacks had the balls, or even the inclination, to say anything other than that Green's club was 'still Rangers'. But Neo-Gers still had to play the victim card.

As well as playing the victim card, the bloggers also used the sectarian one. Leggat's ravings were constantly about how Presbyterianism in Scotland was being eroded by 'sinister forces' that wanted to turn Scotland into a Catholic republic. Other bloggers, like Bill McMurdo, had pretty much the same thing to say. 'Rangers' was a 'Protestant' institution, so any attack on it was an attack on Protestantism.

This desperate attempt to divide all of football along sectarian lines reached its nadir with the way the blame for all their ills fell on just three teams: Celtic, of course, Hibs and Dundee United. The story was that the rest of the teams in the SPL would have been perfectly happy to let Green's new club join them, but they were bullied into complying with the 'bigoted agenda' of Celtic, Hibs and Dundee United. The fact that Dundee United was once called Dundee Hibernian was not lost on The People and this was the name that they began to use when talking about United.

The backs-to-the-wall defiant stance of The People seemed to be working. They were all singing from the same hymn sheet in condemning their imagined enemies and in supporting the myth that Rangers never died. But would this togetherness last? In early February it received its first test.

As soon as the draw was made for the next round of the Scottish Cup and Neo-Gers was paired with Dundee United you just knew there was going to be trouble. No sooner had the balls been drawn than the calls came for a boycott. Green almost straightaway decided to keep The People onside and refused to accept his allocation of tickets for Tannadice.

Green had sung a different song back in September, when his team was facing Motherwell at Ibrox in the League Cup. He said that Motherwell was not 'anti-Rangers' and had been pressured into voting against Neo-Gers getting into the SPL. He said of that meeting,

> What we have to understand is not everyone in that room wanted Rangers out of that league and I know – because I could see glints in eyes – which ones were happy and which ones were not. We know that only half of those clubs wanted Rangers out of that league. I believe that a number of the clubs were bounced into it.[6]

I wonder who he considered was responsible for 'bouncing' them, as if we didn't know! He also came out with a strange phrase, 'We understand we have to suffer the punishment for the sins of the forefathers'.[7] Perhaps this was a sop to McMurdo's and Leggat's Protestantism. After all, the whole Reformation was based on Original Sin and The Fall. (No, not Mark E Smith's band – go and read Genesis in the Bible!) It looked as if Green was prepared to go to any lengths to suck up to The People.

Back to the Dundee United game and, strangely, not all of the media was on Green's side. Mark Hateley, predictably, spoke about Dundee United's 'hypocrisy,'[8] but Keith Jackson felt that Green was pandering to an extremist element.[9] The People almost overwhelmingly backed the boycott but the voices of dissent in the Fourth Estate did not bode well for the future.

Tam Cowan summed up what everybody else felt:

> Did Dundee Utd allow Rangers' debts to spiral out of control? Did Dundee Utd flog the Ibrox club to Craig Whyte for a quid? Did Dundee Utd drag the Govan side into administration by refusing to cough up PAYE and NI to HMRC? Of course not. So why is the Tannadice club apparently being blamed for Rangers ending up in Division Three?
>
> Surely it's time for everyone at Ibrox to stop playing the victim card and start realising that the club's demise was all their own doing?

> This boycott is a wee result for the Dundee Utd fans. With no
> Rangers fans at Tannadice, they won't have to listen to all that
> whingeing about every man and his dug trying to put them out
> of business.[10]

They had even more to whinge about when it emerged that the
Dundee United fans were going to wear Craig Whyte masks to the
match. Of course, most of the Ne-Gers supporters would be
boycotting but a couple of hundred were expected to turn up
regardless so concerns were expressed by the Rangers Supporters
Association about the possibility of violence.[11] And who would be
causing this violence, pray tell? As usual, the Ibrox mob were ready
with the excuses, trying to blame everybody else for the bad
behaviour of their own supporters.

Winding up opposition fans, and teams for that matter, is
something that happens at all football matches. Normal people find
it hilarious when inflatable sheep are brandished at Aberdeen
supporters, including the Aberdeen supporters themselves. The
lower leagues are especially good for this kind of thing, where
smaller stadiums mean that wind-ups are more easily seen and heard.

I remember away back in the early 1980s it was reported in the
newspapers that Queen of the South's veteran goalkeeper, Allan Ball,
had been found guilty of stealing perfume from Boots. He must have
known what was coming that Saturday at Palmerston when
opposition fans called down to him things like, 'You're smelling nice
today, Allan!' and 'Is that Chanel No. 5 you're wearing?' Ball, who
could lose the nut with the best of them, took it all in good spirit.

Sometimes, however, this banter can take a dark turn and deserves
to be pilloried and stamped out; for example, chants about the Ibrox
Disaster, racist abuse of players, the sectarian abuse suffered by Neil
Lennon and, going back a bit, the shouts of 'murderer' that greeted
Sam English everywhere in Scotland. For the most part, though, the
wind-ups can often be more entertaining than the game itself!

Supporters, and even the clubs themselves, can go overboard in
complaining about perceived insults. Our media have fallen over
themselves to make Celtic the ones that constantly do this but, in
fact, it's The People that greet and moan about every little thing.
They even invent things to be offended over, such as the doctored

video on YouTube, which apparently shows Neil Lennon calling folk 'Orange bastards' and throwing a plastic bottle at the crowd. It's quite easy to edit a couple of videos together to get the same kind of result but The People are desperate to believe that it's true.

Even given The People's predilections for violence and being easily offended it would take a special kind of half-cut moron to be driven to a frenzy by the sight of a Craig Whyte mask! 'Look what he did to our club,' would be the answer to what they were offended about. But what did he do? Apparently the team they were following was still Rangers and Peter Lawwell had conspired to throw them into the Third Division; where does Craig Whyte come into it?

In reality the Neo-Gers supporters groups knew as well as

the rest of us that the small crowd going to Tannadice was probably looking for trouble. Moaning about Craig Whyte masks was just getting the excuses in early!

As it turned out, 365 supporters decided to buy tickets directly from Dundee United and attend the match. As far as we know there wasn't any trouble but these folk were derided as 'scabs' by many bloggers and on newspaper forums. Not much was said about this small band of rebels in the newspapers, other than the fact that they were at the match. It showed, however, that perhaps all was not well among The People and, if anything else happened, then there might end up being a bigger group of rebels than the one that turned up at Tannadice.

More worryingly for The People was the story that Ross Blyth, vice-president of the Rangers Supporters Assembly, had to tender his resignation of said body after being caught trying to sneak into Tannadice after advising everyone else to boycott the match![12] Could it be that the supporters groups were only paying lip service to Green's regime?

9
Justice Tonight

February also saw the publication of Lord Nimmo-Smith's long-awaited report on whether or not Rangers had broken the rules and what punishment, if any, they should receive. This inquiry had been the subject of feverish speculation for months, everyone convinced that it was going to go against Rangers. After all, the evidence was there for all to see.

There were many blogs that called for Rangers to be stripped of any titles they had won during the EBT years. It was a cut-and-dried case; side letters had been used on top of normal contracts to sign players, which, otherwise, Rangers could not have afforded. And so Rangers were able to steamroller their way to the title on more than just a couple of occasions.

It was like a team fielding fifteen-year-olds in a competition for under-twelve children. I've seen this happening on quite a few occasions. When you complain nothing gets done about it, while the man in charge of the cheating team, dressed in regulation puffy jacket, swears blind that the six-foot-two lad with the five-o'clock shadow is in Primary 7. The guy in charge usually just shrugs and asks if you want him to demand to see birth certificates. When you answer yes he then turns on you, as if you're the cheat!

There was also the scandal of the Under-16s World Cup final, held at Hampden in 1989. Scotland, believe it or not, had actually made it to this final and faced Saudi Arabia. The Saudi team practically all had beards, prompting claims that there were hardly any of them under the age of sixteen. The match ended in a draw, with the Saudis winning the penalty
shoot-out.

The Saudi team later went out in Glasgow to celebrate their win. There were stories of them flashing ID to prove that they were over 21 to get into nightclubs! Needless to say, however, nothing at all was done about this cheating.

Or what about the big Champions League scandal of 1993? You

know; the one that Rangers supporters have bored everyone with ever since? Marseille was found to have bribed a French league team to take it easy against the Marseille players in their next game so that they could focus and be ready for the Champions League final. Marseille were stripped of their French League title and thrown into the second tier. They still got to hold onto the European Cup, though.

The one that bleats loudest about this injustice is Mark Hateley, who insists that he was offered a bribe to miss a game and questions his sending off against Bruges. Strangely, however, he saw nothing wrong in the double contracts at Rangers and cast doubt on the whole integrity of the Nimmo-Smith inquiry.[1]

I predicted that the outcome of the Nimmo-Smith inquiry would be the same as most other inquiries: nothing. After all, this was Rangers we were talking about, the Establishment team. Who would dare to try to wrest trophies from its cold, dead hands? I fully expected the report to say that 'a big boay dun it an' ran away'.

The People were convinced, just like most others, that Nimmo-Smith was going to decide against their old team. They were ready to decry everything he was going to say. Jabba, before he left the Record, had demanded that the inquiry be dropped, given the result of the First Tier Tribunal.[2] Bloggers and their pals in the papers all prepared for the worst.

Green, of course, employed the old *doublethink* yet again. He refused point blank to have anything to do with the inquiry, citing the fact that it had nothing to do with him or his club. And yet, he promised The People that the titles would be going nowhere. He had bought the history and he was keeping it. It wouldn't matter what Nimmo-Smith had to say; as far as he and The People were concerned they had won them fairly and they would still count them in their tally, no matter what anyone said.

On the Neo-Gers blogs one theme was constant: Rangers were the victims in the EBT scandal as well as the tax payer. A comparison was drawn with the alleged situation at Celtic in the bad old days. The allegation was that the families in charge of Celtic used to downplay attendance figures and cream off the extra money into their own pockets. The argument of the Neo-Gers bloggers was that

Rangers had suffered in the same way.

This argument, however, was completely disingenuous. If the stories about what happened at Celtic were true, then money that should have gone into the team was being stolen. At Rangers, on the other hand, money was stolen from the state to help maintain the success of the team. The two situations were hardly analogous.

At last, Nimmo-Smith's report was published and everyone was left dumbstruck. Yes, Rangers was guilty of using side-letters to conceal extra payments. Yes, Rangers was guilty of keeping these supplementary contracts a secret from the authorities. But, amazingly, Nimmo-Smith concluded that no sporting advantage had been gained. It was an incredible decision and everybody pored over the text to try to make sense of it.

The closer everyone looked, the more it seemed that Nimmo-Smith's hands were tied. Sandy Bryson, the Head of Registrations at the SFA, gave evidence that pretty much left Nimmo-Smith no room for manoeuvre. He said that a player's registration with the SFA remained valid right up until the player left their current club. It didn't matter if any breach had occurred; the registration stood. In other words, under SF

A rules the Rangers players could not be found ineligible to play, no matter what.

Sandy Bryson was right at the centre of the Jorge Cadete scandal. He was the Head of Registrations then as well and was instrumental in making sure that Cadete wasn't eligible to play for Celtic. Strangely, back then it was imperative that all the boxes were ticked in the right places before a player could be eligible. Apparently, by 2012/13 he had changed his mind about the minutiae of eligibility being important.

This was also the character that advised Celtic that Sion FC had done nothing wrong and that the SFA would not be appealing on Celtic's behalf. Celtic had to take the case to UEFA themselves, with the result that Sion was found guilty of fielding ineligible players. So it seems that Bryson had all the qualifications needed to be a credible, expert witness, especially if you were a Rangers supporter!

Nimmo-Smith was also hide-bound by the First Tier Tax Tribunal's findings. This showed the fundamental ridiculousness of the SPL case at that time. Any inquiry of this sort should have been postponed until a final decision had been reached in the tax case. If Rangers were found guilty in the tax case, then they would be guilty of gaining an unfair sporting advantage and no amount of SFA smokescreens would help.

It was obvious that the timing of this investigation was crucial. All Nimmo-Smith would have to go on would be the FTTT outcome. Given this, it appears in hindsight that this was exactly what was intended to happen. Contrary to what the press and the bloggers were telling us, this was not a witch hunt; it was, in fact, a whitewash.

Of course, we were told that Rangers and, by association, Neo-Gers, had been exonerated. Our newspapers made out that all Rangers had been guilty of was an 'administrative error'. This made it sound as if Rangers, in fact, had been guilty of nothing. This, of course, ignored the £250,000 fine that Nimmo-Smith had imposed.

The Daily Record called for resignations from the SPL board and from the SFA. They even demanded that 'Rangers' be put straight 'back' into the SPL! Mark Hately, of course, was right in the van of these calls. According to him, Neo-Gers should be included in the top tier in any league reconstruction plans. He had this laughable comment to make about the situation, 'Rangers are down in the Third Division but they've done their time.'[3]

And there you had it in a nutshell. Believing in the Big Lie meant believing also that being in Division Three was some sort of punishment. Here was Hateley spouting the party line, trying to tell us that 'Rangers' deserved time off for good behaviour. It was getting harder and harder for any Neo-Gers supporter to admit that they were supporting a new team, what with our media constantly telling them it was 'still Rangers'.

He continued with his theme:

> It's all about saving Scottish football. If we carry on the way we are going, in two or three years' time – even if Rangers win the leagues and get back – it could be too late by then. If you were to take Real Madrid out of Spanish football, what would it be like? A one-horse race and nobody shows any interest or puts any investment into a one-horse race. Sporting integrity is to save the football clubs.[4]

So Hateley's idea of sporting integrity is that certain teams are too big to fail under any circumstances. If those teams go into liquidation, then the rules are to be applied differently. Other clubs would have to start over anew but not the chosen few; they are sacrosanct and can never die. Have you ever heard anything so ridiculous in your life?

According to Hateley's view, and that of others, leagues are a waste of time. Spain should be just about Real Madrid and Barcelona playing each other over and over and over, while Scottish football would see nothing but Celtic and Rangers games for ever anon. Hateley would no doubt argue that this is not what he means at all, but, essentially it is; basically he is saying that in ever country football clubs don't matter outside the big names. We'd be as well packing in the whole thing now.

What should have been happening is that Scottish football took the opportunity to assess what is important in the game. For years one club spent money with reckless abandon, forcing others to follow suit; this absolutely ruined our game. Our football authorities should have been looking at things like wage caps to bring a bit of sanity into the game and make it more competitive. What they decided to do, however, was sit and tap their feet and drum their fingers on their desks, waiting for 'Rangers' to get 'back' into the top tier before making any radical changes. I suppose the nightmare scenario was bringing in a wage cap to make things more equitable and then, a couple of years down the line, a sugar daddy turning up at Ibrox but not being allowed to spend big bucks to steamroller his team to the top!

Back to the judgment itself and Green and Sooperally, no longer called the investigation a 'Mickey-Mouse event' or a 'kangaroo court'. Now Nimmo-Smith was the greatest thing since sliced bread. Sooper said, 'It's what Nimmo Smith does for a living. He makes decisions – and I'd have to say he's very good at it.'[5]

The fine was a joke in itself. It was as if they'd dragged Saddam Hussein's body down from the gallows to try it all over again for other crimes and then fine his corpse while leaving his family to hold onto the wealth and power he had accumulated over the years. What was the point in fining a dead club?

As somebody pointed out on the Daily Record phone-in, there was a huge anomaly in all of this. A £250,000 fine was handed to Oldco Rangers and Neo-Gers declared that it has nothing to do with them. And yet, if any of Oldco Rangers' titles had been stripped Neo-Gers would have been up in arms.[6] Like I keep saying: *doublethink*.

There was one ominous passage in the judgment, however, that augured ill for the future. HMRC would no doubt be appealing the decision of the FTTT and this statement, on Page 24 of the Nimmo-Smith ruling, was bound to have an impact:

> If it had not been intended that the player would directly benefit from the EBT arrangements, then there is no reason to believe that the player would have agreed to accept the overall financial package offered by Oldco.

This is not how EBTs were meant to be used and this finding would add weight to HMRC's case. It also, however, paints Nimmo-Smith's ruling that Rangers gained no sporting advantage as being utterly ridiculous.

Green, instead of celebrating the decision, should have been getting some armour-plating for his back. Both this decision, which everybody was bizarrely claiming as proving Rangers' innocence, and the ruling of the First Tier Tax Tribunal were grist to the mill of the 'Rangers Men' backers. Think about it. After the FTTT ruling even McMurdo, Green's biggest supporter, claimed that it was a vindication of David Murray.[7] There were dark murmurings that administration and, whisper it, liquidation, should never have happened. Where would that leave Green?

10
Something About England

'**Z**e plane! Ze plane!' shouts the wee man, Tattoo, as he rings the old church bell. He runs excitedly down the stairs of the tower to go and meet the plane with his boss.

Ricardo Montalban, dressed in the same immaculate, white suit as his assistant, strolls up to the seaplane to welcome more guests, Tattoo running along beside him, still excited. The people get out of the plane, dragging their luggage, looking around and chattering excitedly. Ricardo shakes the hand of his first guest.

'Welcome, Meester Green, to Fannnntassee Island!'

Charles Green's imagination took flight almost as soon as he got the keys to Ibrox. He bragged that his new club would be better-off financially than Celtic within a year. He said, 'We are in the Third Division and Celtic are in the SPL and what I'd like you to do is promise me at the end of this season, when all the games are played, examine the balance sheets of the clubs and tell me which one is the strongest?'[1]

The reasoning behind this bold, and ungrammatical, assertion was that 'We've not got the debt that any of these clubs have'.[2] That would go down well with all the creditors that he'd shafted! It was also a very simplistic way of looking at things.

As well as having no debt Green's new club had no line of credit either; or any other income as yet, apart from ticket sales. Yes, there would be season tickets and the money from the share issue when it came but there would be outgoings as well. There were wages to be paid; big wages and Green was shouting about getting expensive players in to replace the ones that had buggered off. It looked as if he should buy himself a calculator before shooting his mouth off.

He had hinted at who these expensive replacements might be while Rangers were still in administration and he was waiting for a reply to his CVA proposal. He had apparently lined up nineteen targets, including five that were playing at Euro 2012.[3] By July he seemed to have forgotten about these targets; the press seemed to have forgotten about them too.

After that the fantasies came thick and fast. He announced that Neo-Gers were going to do a money-spinning deal with Adidas. This was big news since Adidas is the biggest sportswear manufacturer in Europe and the second-biggest in the World. Green enthused, 'They said to me we've lost Liverpool and Real Madrid, Rangers will be the biggest club we have. We would have spots in Adidas stores in North America. There are massive brand development opportunities.'[4]

And there was more. Ex-Rangers players Claudio Reyna and Carlos Bocanegra would act as Rangers/Adidas ambassadors, whatever that meant!

Bloggers laughed and derided the whole notion but were denounced as 'Rangers-haters'. Our mainstream media, of course, reported the envisaged deal as if it was actually happening. The People waited, and waited, and waited but no deal appeared. What the hell was going on?

It was February 2013 that Neo-Gers finally signed their deal; not with Adidas, however, but with Puma, which sits a distant third in the sportswear league table. It was certainly not the prestigious deal that Green had promised.

Green said of the deal, 'Rangers and Puma are massive global brands and this relationship will undoubtedly improve the distribution of club merchandise in the UK and overseas.'[5] Not as much as Celtic's ongoing deal with Nike, the World's Number 1!

Nobody in our media mentioned Adidas. It was as if it had never happened. To paraphrase George Orwell in 1984, Neo-Gers made a deal with Puma; Neo-Gers were always going to be making a deal with Puma.

It was also reported that Neo-Gers were going to have some kind of tie-in with the American football team Dallas Cowboys.[6] This was, apparently, going to be of huge financial benefit to both clubs. Again it was left to the Internet Bampots to find out the truth.[7] All it took was a phone call or an e-mail to the Dallas Cowboys to discover that they had no idea what Green was on about. But that wasn't going to stop the fantasies continuing.

One of Green's favourite sayings was that he was not going to leave Ibrox until he heard the music of the Champions League booming out at the stadium.[8] Conversely, he said that his team was never going to play in the SPL, or whatever the top tier might be called in the future. He also decided to add a new mythical element to the Big Lie.

> While I'm Chief Executive, Rangers will not play in the Scottish Premier League. [If that situation arose], I would go out to the fans, as we did earlier in the year, when they were consulted as to what division they wanted to play in.
> They wanted to play in the Third Division and we as investors listened to them and were happy to do that.[9]

This, of course, ignored the fact that he had gone barging into the SPL offices demanding that his new team be placed there. And if the Third Division was where they all wanted to be then why the hell were they lashing out at all and sundry and calling for a boycott of Tannadice? Nobody in our media, however, bothered to contradict him.

So how was he going to get into Europe? Well, he had a plan. That plan involved moving to England. As usual, this was couched in defiant, backs-to-the-wall language. It was to be Derry's Walls all over again! Green promised to have it out with UEFA; after all, why were Welsh teams allowed into English leagues and not Scottish? Obscure facts about women's football were cited as precedents as well. The People geared up for the fight.

It would only take a short time for Neo-Gers to climb from the Conference League to take its 'rightful place' among the Manchester Uniteds, Arsenals and Liverpools of this world. The TV money would be flooding in from Neo-Gers' 'worldwide fan-base' and, before too long, the club would be dominating European football. Nothing was going to stand in their way; if anyone tried then The People were ready for the battle.

Unfortunately, all the girded loins in the world couldn't change the fact that the whole idea was nothing but a pipe-dream. Despite the bravado, nobody in England wanted them. Green might have been ready for a fight but there was no enemy for him to battle against. Nobody came out and told him to 'Beat it!' so there was no hate figure for him to concentrate the fury of The People upon.

62

What stood in his way was the fact that nobody in England explicitly invited his club to 'come on down'. Yes, there were noises about 'The Old Firm' being able to do well in England but nobody that mattered made any comment whatsoever. Lack of interest and apathy are hard enemies to fight against so the whole idea just petered out, but not before Green had managed to make a complete arse of himself.

'I don't believe the Premier League are hostile towards it because I think it's a generalisation,' Green said. 'Speak to Manchester United. They are not hostile to Rangers joining,' he added.[10] Unfortunately, Manchester United refuted his claims. 'We are not in favour of it at all. Our view is it's the English Premier League and should remain that way,' said Phil Townsend, a spokesman for United.[11]

Equally unfortunately, Green just couldn't keep his mouth shut. He started banging on about how Barcelona and Real Madrid would want his club in their league. He also derided Spanish teams like Getafe, asking who Barcelona would rather play; Getafe or Neo-Gers. Not only that but folk in the Middle East, Asia and the Far East all wanted to see the big clubs, including Neo-Gers.[12] Rather magnanimously he included Celtic in these plans for world domination.

The Daily Record, of course, fought Green's corner. Mark Hateley waxed lyrical about how Neo-Gers would be welcomed with open arms,[13] while all manner of English has-beens were wheeled out to say that Green's team would fit in well. The Neo-Gers bloggers, meanwhile, were convinced that the fact that they waved Union flags all the time was all it would take to get into the English Premiership. The rest of us just laughed!

Despite Green's best efforts none of his ramblings came anywhere near those of David Leggat for sheer lunacy. He had swallowed whole all the hype about Craig Whyte being responsible for everything from the Cold War to the Bubonic Plague and honestly believed that Whyte was going to end up in prison. What crime was he going to be arrested for; being bad to Rangers? I suppose in Leggat's mind, and that of his readership, that was a crime bigger than anything Hitler, Joseph Stalin or Pol Pot could ever have committed.

And so Leggat's dreams took wings. Once Whyte was safely

banged up in the Big House (no, not that one, I'm talking about prison) then his deal with Ticketus would be null and void. According to Leggat, this would mean that everything would magically go back to the way it was. David Murray would own Rangers again, administration and liquidation would never have happened and Rangers would be in the SPL. And I'm not joking; Leggat was perfectly serious about all this. Bobby Ewing was going to step out of the shower and tell The People that it had all been just a horrible nightmare.[14]

His fantasy continues with the statement that Rangers' ten-point deduction 'gifted the title' to Celtic. This, of course, ignores the fact that Celtic actually won by twenty points, but let's go with Leggat's fevered imagination. In this scenario Rangers would have won the SPL in 2012. It would also 'cast doubt' on Celtic's upcoming second successive title. Everything would be moonlight and roses, beyond even Green's wildest dreams.

Probably, in Leggat's wee world, the bank would get to keep the money while Ticketus would chase after Craig Whyte to recoup their loss. So Rangers would be sitting at the top of the tree, no longer in debt to the bank and, with what

we now knew about the First Tier Tax Tribunal, not owing the tax man either. All they needed to do was pay the wee face-painting woman and everything would be fine. Nobody would be able to stand in the way of a debt-free Rangers!

There are so many holes to pick in Leggat's plot that it's difficult to know where to begin. What about the new Ibrox shareholders? What about the hopeless and hapless Sooperally? No wonder Leggat's novel didn't fare too well if the story went anything like that! Even the most benighted individual could see how insane Leggat's ideas were but that didn't stop the feelings behind his dream from growing. Leggat's ramblings helped fuel the paranoia of The People. Maybe they didn't believe all his future dreams but they swallowed whole his ridiculous guff about the 'Stewart Regan-Peter Lawwell-Rod Petrie-SFA Axis and the Neil Doncaster-Peter Lawwell-Eric Riley-Rod Petrie-SPL Axis'.[15]

This was all grist to The People's mill. The whole mythology was now set in stone. The People had saved Rangers, while everybody, the SPL, the SFA, all the other clubs in the SPL and their fans and the media, had done their best to destroy the team. Envy had fed this hatred, which was still ongoing, and meant that 'Rangers' was going to have to fight to get 'back where it belonged'.

The most enduring fantasy, however, was the Big Lie itself, which, unfortunately, was going to bring its own problems.

11
Play to Win

'RANGERS has become the first football club in the world to launch a crossbar challenge with a mind-blowing prize of £1 million on offer to a supporter at the end of the season.'[1]

So went the blurb on the Neo-Gers website. All The People got excited about this; not only was it a great competition with a great prize, but it would provide half-time entertainment at Ibrox as well as ploughing some much-needed funds into the Neo-Gers coffers.

To enter the competition, you had to phone, or text, a premium-rate number and answer a simple question, which would be published on the official Neo-Gers website. It would be one of those questions that you get on television programmes; you know the ones, with the choice of three answers, two of which would be mind-numbingly stupid. For example, 'What actor is the new Doctor Who? Is it: A Peter Capaldi, B Julius Caesar or C Skippy the bush kangaroo?' In reality it's no better than a raffle.

So you phone or text the number, get charged a fortune and your name goes into a prize draw. Normally only a complete idiot would give this kind of thing the time of day but this one was different. Instead of the money going into some TV company's bank account a good chunk of it would be going to Neo-Gers. So even if you couldn't afford to buy shares or a season ticket you could still do your bit and have the chance to win a prize as well.

If you were lucky enough to have your name drawn, then you got the chance to try the 'Crossbar Challenge'. This involved kicking a football from the centre spot and trying to hit the crossbar. The first such challenge was going to take place on 23rd September 2012. The prize was going to be £50,000, 'in celebration of Ally McCoist's impending 50th birthday.'[2]

And there was more. Everybody chosen to take part would receive a signed strip, so at least there was some kind of consolation prize. There was also the Grand Finale at the final home game of the season. The competition was going to 'reach unprecedented heights when a lucky supporter will have the chance to win £1 million at the final home game against Berwick Rangers in May – where thousands of fans will undoubtedly be on the edge of their seats to see if the £1 million prize can be secured by hitting the crossbar.'[3]

Everything about the competition, however, was a bit vague. How many shots did you get to hit the crossbar? Who would be eligible for the £1 million – would it be those that had managed to hit the crossbar previously, would all those that had taken part get a chance or would it just be those that phoned in at that particular time? And, apart from the 23rd September, what were the other prizes going to be? Presumably each prize would be announced whenever a new question went up on the site.

There was another consideration: what if you didn't have a ticket for the match? There were plenty of folk that might chance a few quid having a couple of goes at the phone-in competition but didn't have the wherewithal to afford the price of a match ticket. If one of these people were chosen would they be invited to see the game gratis? Would they be made to hide somewhere until their moment of stardom came at half-time and then be flung out of the stadium afterwards? Or maybe they'd be sent their signed strip and then told to 'piss of ya stingy bastard!'

Tam Cowan, among others, wondered where Neo-Gers were getting the money from. He also demonstrated his uncanny knack of saying what the rest of us were thinking. He mused on the possibility of a referee saving the Ibrox team's bacon, not for the first time, and disallowing it if somebody was actually lucky enough to hit the crossbar! He also asked if this was a ploy to recruit a new striker.[4]

Actually, that wasn't a bad idea. If you could hit the crossbar from the centre spot, then surely you could hit the back of the net from outside the goal area? You wouldn't have to be fit or anything as all you would need to do is just stand there. The other players would lump the ball up to you the whole game, while Lee McCulloch and Ian Black 'took care' of the opposition defenders. That had been the standard Ibrox tactic for years!

Anyway, back to the competition itself, and I'm sure Tam Cowan was just asking where Neo-Gers were getting the money from for comic effect. Everybody knows that these competitions are organised by specialised companies, who use the huge profits from the phone calls to pay out prize money, pay the company that hired them and also keep a handsome amount for themselves. This competition would be no different.

The problem was, though, that this competition *was* different. The company running it was called Strathan ME Limited, into whom an intrepid individual by the name of Ecojon decided to do some digging. Unfortunately, he wasn't able to dig very far: his spade hit an obstacle right away. There was no address available for this company, nor was it listed at Companies House. The Terms and Conditions of the competition said that 'All decisions of Strathan ME Limited will be final and binding. No correspondence will be entered into' As Ecojon said, this was 'quite understandable as it would be difficult, if not impossible, to correspond with a mystery company with no apparent address!'[5]

And there's more. Ecojon discovered that the URL for the competition advert and rules was registered to a company in Glasgow, called Matador Creative. Ecojon went on to find out that Matador Creative was in the process of being liquidated!

Surely that's it? Nope. I'll let Ecojon continue:

Well the Matador Creative web page lists Customer services for the competition as 'Call Centre Sales Scotland Ltd' First Floor, 1 Dukes Road, Troon, KA10 6QR. The sole director is Kelly Munro, 35, who was appointed on 3/08/2011. However, Companies House records show that the nature of business is a 'Dormant Company' and that the accounts are overdue.'[6]

So it looked as if anybody that won the competition would be hard-pushed to actually get their hands on a prize. With the company running the competition in liquidation it might give at least one of The People an insight into how the creditors of his dead club felt!

Strangely, there wasn't a big deal made about this competition. (Or maybe not so strangely, considering what Ecojon discovered!) You would imagine the Neo-Gers website would be full of videos showing attempts and describing how close the person was or even pictures of the folk that had had a go, saying what prize they had won and how they'd like to try again. Surely they wanted to get folk excited about the competition and have them phoning multiple times? But there was nothing. In fact, you wouldn't even have been aware of the competition unless you actually went to Ibrox and witnessed it.

'A prize of this value has never been offered in this way in football before and it is another first for Rangers.'[7] With such boasting you'd think they'd want to make more of a big deal about it. Or maybe it was going to be another 'first'; the first football team to refuse to pay out when one of its supporters wins a competition!

It reminds me of the Mel Brooks film, The Producers. If you remember, the two characters get old ladies to buy shares in a play they're going to produce. It's seriously over-subscribed but the whole thing is a scam anyway; produce a flop that closes after its opening night and they don't have to pay out any dividends. The 'Crossbar Challenge' was the same sort of thing; nobody was meant to win.

There's a video on YouTube of the Crossbar Challenge on 4th May 2013. This was the big one; the £1 million challenge![8] We still don't know if this was somebody that had tried before and won their way through to a 'final' or if this was somebody chosen at random in another phone-in. Whatever the case, it's pretty obvious from the video that the guy wasn't meant to hit the crossbar.

For a start, he only got one shot, for Christ's sake! And then there's all the crap going on round about him. The centre circle was crowded with people while behind them, in the other half of the pitch, there were kids having some kind of kick-about. Meanwhile, in front of the guy, over on his right, Broxi Bear was dancing about on the edge of the goal area. And to put the tin hat on it, just before he was about to take his kick, they turned the fucking sprinklers on right in his line of vision! Needless to say, the poor bastard was nowhere near with his effort.

Strangely, nobody has ever asked what happened to all the money that was raked in from this competition. The answer to that probably lies in the fact that I've spoken about before: The People tend to have short arms and deep pockets. No doubt hardly anybody bothered to phone in to answer the stupid questions. Then again, maybe they were showing uncharacteristic sense in refusing to take part in this raffle. Whatever the reason, I've a feeling that there wasn't enough money in the pot to pay out the big-money prizes. No wonder they put so much effort into putting that guy off his shot!

By the end of the 2012-13 season the Crossbar Challenge was just forgotten about. Nobody mentioned it or questioned it but it was one more little chink in the armour of the Ibrox board. Only spivs and crooks would run such a scheme. Subconsciously it was another mark chalked up against those currently running Neo-Gers. 'Real Rangers Men' wouldn't treat the supporters like that, would they?

12
Should I Stay or Should I Go

As 2013 progressed, Sooperally's team got itself into a winning streak. With no cup competitions to take away their focus, Neo-Gers could now concentrate fully on the job in hand: winning Division 3. Fortunately, Sooper had hit on a master plan to achieve this end. He was still tactically ignorant ('Jist punt it up the park, boays!') but he had found a way to actually win games without his team of professionals having to break into too much of a sweat.

It stands to reason that part-time players, who work all week and train in their spare time, are going to be nowhere near as fit as full-time professionals, with their pampered lifestyle, physios, masseurs and dolly-bird wives that won't be banging their ears about the sink needing unblocked. It also stands to reason that such part-time players are going to get tired a lot quicker than their professional counterparts during a ninety-minute match.

This was Sooperally's cunning plan. The Neo-Gers would just run about the pitch like big Jessies for 70 or 80 minutes, not trying overly hard. As long as they defended in numbers everything would be alright. The opposition, however, would be dropping down with cramp, exhaustion, kidney failure, heart attacks and brain fever in the last ten to twenty minutes, while their schoolboy midfielder would be desperately trying to hide the stauner that had suddenly appeared for no reason.

It was then an easy matter for the Neo-Gers players to score a goal or two, especially since the opposition goalkeeper would be fighting to stave off a deep-vein thrombosis from standing about doing nothing during the game. If things were still proving too difficult then the referee was there to send somebody off or point to the penalty spot.

Despite this the Neo-Gers players ran about celebrating as if they'd just won the Champions League. The press, too, went overboard, constantly going on about Lee McCulloch being a 'prolific goalscorer'.

Everything was rosy; it was all 'onwards and upwards' and 'coming down the road' as far as things on the pitch were concerned. Off-field, however, things were not looking too clever.

The story in the Daily Record was that there was disagreement between Sooperally and Charles Green. It seemed that Green had suggested that Ally get rid of Ian Durrant and Kenny McDowall. Apparently, Sooper's own job was under threat and this was going to be the only way he could keep it.[1]

Green had already got rid of a few folk. Pip Yeates, the physiotherapist, the chief scout Neil Murray and hapless striker Fran Sandaza had been shown the door. Murray left after some kind of 'investigation'[2] while Yeates was apparently leaving to focus on his own business.[3] Fran Sandaza leaving was a saga all of its own.

A character called Tommy, a Celtic supporter, phoned Sandaza and pretended to be a football agent in Los Angeles. Tommy had done this sort of thing before, even managing to trick Craig Whyte. Sandaza was led to believe that he was wanted by some major-league team in the USA. Of course, he was keen on the move but he would have to leave Neo-Gers first; could he drag himself away? He most certainly could since he was only there for the money![4]

Usually players hide this kind of thing, even though we all know it's the truth. Whenever a player signs for a new team they appear in the papers, telling us all how it's their 'dream move' and how they've wanted to play for that particular team their whole life. We all know it's a load of shite but we all play along. It was a bit hard to take players seriously, however, when it was their 'dream move' to sign for a team playing in the fourth tier!

Now Sandaza had come out and told us the truth. We all got a good laugh but, of course, The People didn't see the funny side at all. Sandaza's days were numbered and it wasn't long before he got his P45. He didn't get his move to America but he did get a move upwards, to CD Lugo in the Spanish Second Division.

Now it looked like Green wanted to get rid of some more people. This, of course, meant tension, to say the least, between Green and McCoist.

This tension became built up in the media as a huge boardroom struggle. On one side was Charles Green, on the other was Malcolm Murray. What was behind this struggle either nobody knew or nobody was saying. And quite who was on Murray's side nobody was sure, but he seemed to be hanging on in there.

Attempts had already been made to get rid of Murray, including demands from Blue Pitch Holdings and even Charles Green himself, who at one point threatened to walk if Murray wasn't forced out.[5] They seemed to have patched up their differences by the end of February and things looked like getting back to normal. But there was more to come.

Not only was there the reported tension between Green and McCoist but it seemed that there was a split developing in the boardroom. On one side were Green and his supporters; on the other were Malcolm Murray and his supporters, including Walter Smith. The media was in a quandary; it was pretty obvious who they supported in this split but they found it hard to come straight out and say.

Walter Smith's credentials as a 'Real Rangers Man' were, of course, impeccable; but what about Malcolm Murray? He had apparently been a season-ticket holder at Ibrox for many years and he was a good friend of Smith so that was enough to convince the agnivores. But how were they going to attack Green after building him up for so long? And then help came from an unexpected source.

There had been rumours about Charles Green almost as soon as he appeared on the scene. Nearly everybody thought at first that he was merely acting as a front man for someone else. As time went on, however, the press was dazzled by his 'Yorkshire bluntness' and the stories disappeared. The 'Internet Bampots,' though, wouldn't let it lie.

Green obviously had some kind of communication with Craig Whyte; anybody that wanted to buy the club during administration would have to have had conversations with the guy that owned the place. When things were whittled down to a competition between Green and the Blue Knights, both sides claimed that Whyte had promised them his shares. All well and good but the smell from the deal done between Green and the administrators, whom Craig Whyte had appointed, remember, suggested something deeper between Whyte and Green.

There were suggestions on blogs that Green was actually a front for Whyte and that the latter was still involved at Ibrox. Even some Neo-Gers fans were involved in thinking in this way. The mainstream media, however, ignored it; it was all just rumour and innuendo, after all. All the papers offered us was stories about companies that both

Green and Whyte had been involved in, even tenuously. This was hardly explosive stuff. Most businessmen are bound to be connected in some way or another as they grub about trying to make as much money as they can.

It was Craig Whyte himself that finally put the lid on Green's metaphorical coffin. As early as October 2012, Whyte had been saying that he introduced Green to Duff and Phelps and that he had set the deal up.[6] Green, of course, denied this and claimed that Whyte was lying. And then, in April, came the bombshell. Whyte released documents that showed him as a director of Sevco 5088. The documents all had Charles Green's signature on them! He also released tape recordings of conversations that clearly demonstrated that he was speaking the truth.[7]

At first Green tried to be too clever, claiming that he'd strung Whyte along. He and Imran Ahmad, apparently, had signed up Whyte to Sevco 5088 in order to buy the assets of Rangers. Whyte set the deal up with Duff and Phelps and then Green, with bluff, Yorkshire sleight of hand, set up another company, Sevco Scotland, to buy the assets without involving Whyte. The actual transaction with Duff and Phelps is listed as the sale being made simply to 'Sevco'. Green's days, however, were numbered.

Anyone who has a child will remember one of the pitfalls of pushing a pram outside: it's an absolute magnet for dog shit! No matter how careful you are, or how much you check the wheels, you can be virtually guaranteed to find a trail of shite through the house when you get back. It's all over the hall carpet and into the living room, where you were letting your auntie see the baby. Then you went back through the hall to wheel the pram into your bedroom to let the baby finish his or her snooze. You can smell it everywhere and you frantically try to clean it before baby wakes up, wanting to be fed. Even in places where you can't see or smell it you know it's there.

Craig Whyte was just like that pram wheel. Such a good job had been made of demonising him that the slightest association with him meant that you were befouled. It appeared that Green had more than just a slight association and it was going to take a lot more than a scrubbing brush and a bottle of Dettol to remove that taint.

There was nothing else for it; Green was pushed out the door. He put a face on it, saying he was resigning for the good of the club blah…blah…, but we all knew that his position had become untenable. Both he and his 'P*** friend,' Imran Ahmad, were also going to be investigated by the Serious Fraud Office.

Ahmad, meanwhile, had his own, personal troubles. He was accused of posting unflattering, and downright hostile, things about Sooperally and Walter Smith on a Neo-Gers blog. No evidence was presented but it was claimed that the posts came from Ahmad's online account at Ibrox. Not surprisingly, Ahmad soon followed Green out the door.

The board at Ibrox announced that it would be instituting an 'independent' inquiry into the claims that Whyte was connected to the new club. The SFA, of course, decided that it would not now need to conduct an enquiry of its own; they would wait and see what the result of Neo-Gers' enquiry was.

The downfall of Green caused a certain rift between the Neo-Gers bloggers. Both Leggat and Bill McMurdo had been unanimous in asserting that Green had been the victim of 'dark forces,' whether as part of a power struggle within Ibrox or as part of the imagined campaign being waged against the Ibrox club by the whole world and its mother, led, of course, by Peter Lawwell. The Ahmad affair, however, seemed to shift Leggat into the anti-Green camp. This would become significant later.

Then a video appeared on the internet of Neo-Gers Chairman, Malcolm Murray, staggering drunkenly out of a restaurant. It soon emerged that it was Brian Stockbridge, the financial director at Neo-Gers and one of Leggat's erstwhile Three Musketeers, who had taken this video. He denied, however, that he had leaked the video. Seemingly it had been shown to the board as part of an effort to encourage Murray to 'cut back on his socialising.'[8] The big question now was: who had leaked the video?

Of course, to Leggat there was only one suspect; Imran Ahmad. In every blog he wrote he had something to say about Ahmad, who had now replaced Graham Spiers as Leggat's bête noir. According to Leggat, Green had just been a front-man for Ahmad, who, he alleged, was responsible for everything wrong in the world. As he did with Spiers, Leggat became totally obsessed and could scarcely speak of anything else.

There was something, however, that everybody seemed to be ignoring, as I pointed out on my own blog:

Now, Stockbridge has denied categorically that he uploaded this video to the internet; so who did? In this technological age there is no need for a video taken on a mobile phone to be uploaded to a computer and rendered into a compatible format for everyone to see. With a modern phone it is possible, in fact, simple, to just plug a cable into the phone, attach the other end to a TV or monitor and show everybody your video in widescreen, HD glory! So, essentially, there was no need for copies of Stockbridge's video to exist, unless he made a back-up on his own computer. He could have shown his video, everyone would have shaken their heads and tut-tutted and another nail would have gone into Murray's coffin.

So what, exactly, am I getting at here? Obviously, if Stockbridge is right and he didn't upload the video to the internet then somebody else had a copy. There was no necessity whatsoever for anybody to have a copy of this video and the only way they could have got it was from Stockbridge. I can imagine the scenario being the same as in secondary schools up and down the country. Teenagers very rarely have their mobile phones out of their hands and are always ready to record embarrassing incidents. These videos are sent from mobile to mobile so everybody can get a laugh and then usually end up on YouTube. Equally, Stockbridge's video was probably shared so they could all look, laugh and comment on the state that Murray was in![9]

So, even though Stockbridge might not have personally put the video on the internet he was, ultimately, responsible. Whatever the plan had been, however, it backfired. Nobody was bothered about Murray being drunk; it was the sneaky bastard that had made the video public that deserved to be condemned, whoever he was.

And so Murray still clung on, even though it seemed everyone wanted rid of him, apart from his friend Walter Smith. Finally, however, the investors had had enough and, at a meeting in London, he was removed as Chairman. His replacement? None other than his pal, Mr Dignity himself, Walter Smith!

This, of course, was welcomed by all the supporters of Neo-Gers. Bill McMurdo looked forward to a united boardroom; if anyone could bring the warring factions together, it was Smith.[10] Leggat, as usual, went overboard, comparing Smith to Churchill and looking forward to victory in the fight against…well…everybody![11]

Our media now had to change the whole story of the Big Lie. They had spent months telling us how Green had 'saved' Rangers; now he was the bad guy, so a new myth was needed. Green had not 'saved Rangers' at all. That privileged position was now allotted to the supporters. The story now was that Rangers had nearly died but the fans had rallied round to save the club. Of course, The People lapped this up.

Keith Jackson, in the Daily Record, decided to pat down the dirt covering Green, just to make sure he didn't get back up. He told us how Neo-Gers could have been placed into the SPL and that eight - yes eight - clubs had been ready to rubber-stamp their admittance. That was until Green turned up with his prospectus, which proclaimed, 'We Are Rangers.' It was Green's arrogant demands that put everyone off and led to the club being 'demoted' to Division 3.[12]

And so, Green and Ahmad were gone; only Stockbridge remained of Leggat's Three Musketeers. The 'Rangers Men' had triumphed, it appeared. Surely everything would be fine now at Ibrox, wouldn't it? Well, this would be a bloody short book if it was!

13
Police and Thieves

Before he left for good, there were a couple of things that Charlie Boy had to attend to. The first one I'm just surmising, but surely he kept his promise to himself and listened to Zadok the Priest over the Ibrox loudspeakers before he buggered off? The second was to let everyone know to whom he would be passing on his shares.

Green's shares were tied-in and he couldn't sell them until December 2013. In the meantime, however, there was nothing to stop him handing over his proxy until his nominated successors could get their mitts on the actual shares. The first of his inheritors were going to be the Easdale brothers, a fact that didn't go down too well with many of The People.

The problem was that the Easdales had a rather unsavoury reputation, whether deserved or not. Sandy Easdale was convicted in 1997 for VAT fraud and served a prison sentence for his crime. That, however, hardly qualified him for gangster status; many so-called respectable businessmen have been convicted of much worse. Despite the many allegations made against him and his brother, James, not a thing has ever been proven. It seems that they are what they appear to be: two men that own a bus company and a fleet of taxis.

That, however, didn't stop me and others from taking the piss. Mud sticks and it has to be said that both Easdale brothers dress like Charles Endell from the TV series Budgie and look as if they'd be more at home in ringside seats at a boxing match rather than in a football team's directors' box. It also didn't stop The People from worrying whether they were 'fit and proper persons' or not. And it certainly didn't stop Leggat from casting aspersions that they were part of some clique involving Charles Green and Imran Ahmad.[1]

The other intended recipient of Charlie Boy's shares was a hedge-fund company called Laxey Partners. This lot didn't seem to worry The People much, but they should have done. This company had a reputation of disrupting businesses and forcing through payouts to shareholders, whether the business needed the money for other things or not. Laxey could cause a lot more trouble than anything the Easdales could possibly do, but nobody seemed interested. I suppose the Easdales were more visible and high-profile.

And an even more high-profile character was on the horizon, if the rumours were to be believed; Dave King was coming back. King, unlike Whyte, did have wealth off the radar. He had invested £20m during David Murray's reign and had lost this when Rangers was liquidated. Now he was coming back to buy up shares and take his place as the main player at the top of the marble staircase.

Strangely, King had stood beside HMRC in rejecting Green's CVA proposal. I'm assuming that what he was owed was his £20m so if the CVA proposal had paid out the full 8p in the £1 he stood to get £160,000. That might not be much to a multi-millionaire but it's better than bugger all! It makes you wonder why he rejected it. Then again, maybe he thought there was going to be a proper sale of the assets!

At any rate, he was facing a huge tax evasion case in South Africa, which was the reason everyone gave for him not stepping in to save Rangers. The justice system in South Africa is just as slow as everywhere else in the world so in 2013 it was still hanging over him like a Sword of Damocles. So what was different now? How was he going to be able to afford to buy shares in Neo-Gers?

David Leggat, of course, had all the answers. According to him, all King's troubles were over and his assets outside of South Africa had been unfrozen.[2] Now he was ready to plough all his millions into Neo-Gers. Leggat was almost orgasmic at the prospect.

Bill McMurdo was also keen on King getting involved, seeing a united board with King, James Easdale and Brian Stockbridge all working together for the good of the club.[3] This was all part-and-parcel of McMurdo's wish for a modern, forward-looking club, devoid of brown brogues.

Leggat, on the other hand, wanted 'Real Rangers Men' at Ibrox. This was his reason for wanting King in the boardroom; the man was a 'diehard bluenose' and had proven this with his previous investment in David Murray's old club.

This became a theme on the blogs. McMurdo was completely

behind Green all the way and wanted him back. He was desperate to keep out the old-school types; the ones that had destroyed Rangers in the first place. Leggat, on the other hand, was keen for the old Rangers to come back. Walter Smith was already in place; now he wanted King there as well. This rift was to become bigger as time went on.

It seemed that many in the Neo-Gers support, or at least the most vocal section, agreed with Leggat. In fact, they went further than Leggat, tarring everyone on the board with the same shit-stained brush that had been used on Green. It didn't matter if it was Green, Ahmad, the Easdales or whoever; they could all fuck off as far as they were concerned.

Words like 'spivs' and 'crooks' started to appear; not just on blogs but on old, smeggy bedsheets displayed at Ibrox. Green had been nothing but a conman and a thief, they said and they doubted whether his replacements would be any better. Of course, it didn't help matters when Green buggered off to a chateau in France!

Green only had himself to blame. When he bought the assets he could have admitted that he was starting a new club from the ashes of Rangers. It might have taken a while but he would have tempted The People back eventually, especially since his team would be playing at Ibrox. Instead, Green decided to pretend that his new club was still Rangers so as to have a guaranteed fanbase. It was a dangerous game to play.

Since the media went along with Green's charade The People were easily duped into thinking that the club currently at Ibrox was, indeed, Rangers. That being the case, it was hardly surprising when they decided they wanted 'Real Rangers Men' in charge, instead of folk that the papers were telling them were all linked to the Antichrist, Craig Whyte.

Although there was no war as such and the Easdales seemed perfectly happy for King to come on board, our media didn't quite see it that way. To them King was the Messiah, come to save 'Rangers' from the 'spivs' and 'crooks' associated with Charles Green. They could hardly hold King up as a paragon of probity so our media went on the offensive against the board instead. Whenever the Easdales were mentioned they were always called 'James Easdale and his convicted-fraudster brother, Sandy.' The agnivores did this with a perfectly straight face, seemingly unaware of the irony of talking like this about Sandy Easdale when, next to their hero, King, he was a saint in comparison!

The rumours about Dave King, meanwhile, proved to be totally unfounded and he failed to put in any sort of appearance. It seemed that all his assets were still tied up by the South African Revenue Service and, despite what Leggat might say, he was in no position to be throwing money around.

The ghost of King, however, still hovered around in the background like a fart left behind in a lift, standing as a symbol for all those that wanted 'Real Rangers Men' on the board. The battle lines had been drawn.

Still, for anyone worried about the involvement of the Easdales or King, things could have been a lot, lot worse. At the end of June taped conversations appeared online, no doubt posted by Charlotte Fakes, letting everyone hear a conversation among Brian Stockbridge, Imran Ahmad and Craig Whyte. The conversations are pretty dismissive of Charles Green, whom the three men seem to be setting up as some kind of patsy. Staggeringly, this chimed with what Leggat had been saying for weeks; *in vino veritas* right enough!

Poor old Sooperally gets it in the neck as well. Craig Whyte says, 'McCoist is useless. McCoist is fucking useless...'[4] Whyte also explains that Jelavic had started refusing to play and that was why he was sold. Interestingly, Sooperally had agreed with Whyte about this sale.

The most disturbing aspect, however, was the plan to get investment from a guy called Rafat Rizvi. Now this guy *was* a crook. He was on Interpol's 'most wanted' list for 'corruption, money laundering and banking crime' in Indonesia.[5] Apparently Rizvi and a business partner stole £907m from Bank Century in Indonesia. That makes Dave King look small-time and certainly puts Sandy Easdale's VAT fraud in the shade!

In the tapes Ahmad tells Whyte that he already has £5.5m of Rizvi's money, although the majority of these funds were supplied by Rizvi's 'mates'. Throughout the comversations Stockbridge is worried about anyone finding out about their connections to Rizvi. Ahmad, however, puts his mind at rest and tells him just to deny everything. Once they've got Rizvi's cash then they're going to try

81

and ditch him.[6] They planned also to ditch Green, which is the opposite of the story that Green was putting about. Maybe Leggat was right and Ahmad was the mastermind behind the whole operation!

Stockbridge had this to say about Rizvi, 'He's a nice guy. I speak to him but I wouldn't do a deal with him.'

Again, Ahmad reassures him, 'We'll take his money but that's it.'[7]

With all these shady dealings being revealed it was hardly surprising that The People started shouting about 'spivs' and 'crooks'. Who was to say that this guy Rizvi hadn't been involved and maybe was still involved? After all, nobody knew who the hell was behind Margarita and Blue Pitch. It made the need for 'Real Rangers Men' all the more urgent.

14
Lightning Strikes
(Not Once but Twice)

In June 2013 something happened that momentarily took everyone's attention away from all the trouble at Ibrox: Hearts went into administration. Since the season was over they couldn't be docked any points so they would be starting the new season with a 15-points deduction, making them favourites for relegation.

It was the collapse of Ukio Bankas, the Lithuanian bank owned by Vladimir Romanov that was causing the bother. Not only was the bank part-owner of Hearts it was also its biggest creditor, causing no end of problems for the Gorgie club. There was a great deal of confusion over how administration was to be dealt with since it came under both Scottish and Lithuanian law. As if things weren't bad enough!

Hearts had been unable to pay its players and its inability to pay a tax bill was the straw that broke the camel's back. Drastic cuts had to be made and the whole team was put up for sale. It looked as if this might not be enough and there was every danger that the liquidators might be arriving at Tynecastle. It might be thought that liquidation was nothing to worry about any more, after what had happened at Ibrox. Hearts, however, was not Rangers. Alex Salmond might be a Hearts fan but that meant nothing in the grand scheme of things.

There was even more to worry about when Hearts were blocked from appointing their preferred administrators, KPMG. Ukio Bankas made sure they got their own administrators in place. This was concerning since Ukio Bankas had a claim on Tynecastle Stadium as security over a £15m loan.[1] Potentially Hearts could end up being evicted and the board selling the Big Issue outside the Co-Op on Dalry Road.

The People were unanimous in what they thought about the situation:

'Let them rot I say let us remember the treatment we received'.

'…watch the machinations for them, they MUST be treated the same way we were.'

'I wonder if they'll get fined the maximum amount-£50,000- by the SFA…'

'To those Hearts fans who revelled in our difficulties last year – GIRFUY.'[2]

McMurdo himself had this to say, 'I'm sure the First Minister will do all he can to help this Scottish institution survive. He would do the same for any Scottish club, wouldn't he…?'[3]

Of course, this guff was all about the myth of Neo-Gers being victimised. I'm sure McMurdo remembers, just like the rest of us, how Alex Salmond tried to intervene with HMRC on Rangers' behalf.[4] As to the £50,000 fine, which Hearts didn't actually get, that was easily explained by the SFA:

Rangers were placed into administration following the deliberate non-payment of social taxes, despite - in the evidence provided - having the money to do so when the decision was first taken to withhold the money. This was not a feature in the Heart of Midlothian or Dunfermline Athletic cases.[5]

And then news emerged of Gary Locke, the Hearts manager looking for a match against Neo-Gers as a fundraiser. This sent The People almost apoplectic. They swarmed all over the Daily Record phone-in, splenetic in their fury.

'Hearts had a cheek even to think about playing against Rangers in a fundraiser when we got no help from them a year ago.'

'Hearts' problems are their own fault.'[6]

84

The contributors to McMurdo's blog went even further:

'BLUE POUND" IS WHAT THEY WANT AFTER THAT
IT'S A CASE OF GO FUCK YOURSELF'.

'Would rather lie in my own pish , read there wankpot forums
and see why we should never forgive or forget, right down to
their management who wanted us dead'.[7]

A Hearts fan decided to risk derision and state the following on
McMurdo's blog:

> I think you'll find the majority of Hearts fans will accept their
> 'punishment' for going into Administration with good grace
> and an acceptance of the consequences of their club's
> mismanagement. Not many at Tynecastle are in denial mode
> or seeking revenge for being caught 'cheating'. Angry, yes, but
> not looking to blame others and certainly not trying to avoid
> appropriate 'punishment'. Problems may arise if we go into
> liquidation and don't get the same, rule breaking, special
> treatment that Rangers got or if we get taken over by
> profiteering liars and cheats, but other than that, I'm sure
> you'll see the majority of Hearts fans behaving with dignity.[8]

Oh dear, they wouldn't like that much, would they? The fact that
it was true made it even harder to stomach. No Hearts fans
marched on Hampden or on the BBC. No death threats were
received at Center 1 with Edinburgh post marks. There were no
demands for help or special treatment and no shouting in the
media about Scottish football facing Armageddon without Hearts.
The behavior of the Hearts supporters was in stark contrast to
that of The People, who blamed everyone outside of Govan for
what had happened to their club.

The sheer arrogance of The People was manifest in this
episode. The myth of the 'same team' had become so strong that
they honestly believed that the other SPL teams had done the
dirty on them. They had been 'thrown out' of the SPL by envious

rivals and left to rot in the lower leagues, while being saddled with 'unfair' fines and transfer embargos. No wonder they all wanted Hearts to die!

Then Gary Locke revealed that he hadn't asked for any help but, instead, had been looking round, before administration even happened, for teams to play friendlies against during the summer. Sooperally was only one of a few that he had contacted. Locke said, 'We will get out of this situation on our own. We have got a great fan base that will help us and we won't be relying on anyone else.'[9]

Well that would certainly put The People's gas at a peep! And, as it turned out, the Hearts fans did rally to the cause and raised funds, not a 'fighting fund,' like that of The People, but a real pile of money that helped to buy Hearts before they went into liquidation. I bet that went down well with the Ibrox hordes!

There is one question that has never been asked: who leaked the story of Gary Locke's request to the press? Obviously there's only one candidate: the recipient of Locke's phone call, Sooperally himself. Surely Sooper wouldn't try to cause trouble like that, would he? After all, it's not like he has a history of being sleekit or anything!

There's one final quote from McMurdo's blog that is extremely interesting in the context of this book:

> Reading these posts Bill shows me a lot of true bears still hurting and angry at the way we're being treated and rightly so! My concern is why is'nt anybody within ibrox showing the same passion or heart? The board and management team are sitting in dignified silence and watching this all happen! Rangers men my arse![10]

What, exactly, was it that folk like this wanted the Neo-Gers board to do? Were they expecting them to lead an assault on the offices at Hampden? The constant references to 'the way we're being treated' showed that The People had not the first idea of what had happened at their club; and didn't want to know either. Like some petulant child that doesn't get its own way, they couldn't listen to reason. And, in the same way that petulant child will just lash out at what it sees as 'injustice', The People were ready for a fight. Anyone that wasn't up for a square go simply wasn't a 'Real Rangers Man'!

The Big Lie, then, didn't just necessitate 'Real Rangers Men' in the Blue Room in order to perpetuate the myth that the new club was still Rangers; it engendered a more worrying trend. As we have already seen, the Big Lie led to The People believing that their club had been badly treated. Since it was the same club, then it shouldn't have had to start over in the bottom tier. The desire for 'Real Rangers Men' at Ibrox was a symptom of this deluded sense of victimisation. They were needed if the 'fight' was going to be taken directly to the 'enemy'.

15
48 Hours

On 4th June 2013 Leggat announced that he was taking a 'wee summer break' and wouldn't be blogging for a while. He said that he was behind in a project he was working on. Some unkind souls suggested that he was going into a drying-out clinic. Some, more unkind, souls suggested that he was going on a massive bender and would be lying, pished out his nut until September. Others, even more unkindly, said that he was paralytic all the time anyway. What do I think? I couldn't possibly comment.

He came back on 30th July, full of piss and vinegar as usual, blaming Imran Ahmad for everything. As he saw it, the only obstacle to Ahmad's schemes was 'the man who stands as a metaphor for integrity, chairman Walter Smith.'[1]

Obviously Leggat hadn't been paying too much attention. Even before he disappeared on his short sabbatical Smith had been mixed up in the boardroom battles. The Easdales, backed by Blue Pitch Holdings, were looking to get rid of Smith's pal, Malcolm Murray, who seemed to be as difficult to shift as dandruff. At one point it was reported that Smith only had forty-eight hours to make up his mind about shoving Murray out the door or face an Emergency General Meeting.[2]

Murray eventually 'resigned' as a director in early July; Walter 'Brutus' Smith, despite all his previous threats to go if Murray was forced out, remained ensconced in his position of chairman. This was the second time he had stabbed his pal in the back; the first being when he nicked Murray's job. So much for integrity!

The main gist of Leggat's blog was, as I have said, Imran Ahmad. In his usual, obsessive way he accused Ahmad of trying to unseat Smith and destabilise Neo-Gers. Why he would want to do this Leggat doesn't say but, then, paranoid delusions tend not to need reasons. He dragged Bill McMurdo into the conspiracy, stating explicitly that he was a dupe of Charles Green, who, in turn, was following orders from Imran Ahmad.

Of course, McMurdo was hardly best pleased by these so-called revelations; in fact, he was absolutely fucking blazing! As well as letting Leggat, and the rest of us, know how he felt about Leggat's fantasies, McMurdo also told us how it was an open secret that Leggat's contact inside Ibrox, 'someone of impeccable integrity and someone who has the good of Rangers in his heart,' as Leggat called him, was none other than our old friend, Jabba![3]

This showed what a hypocrite Jabba was. Not only had he completely changed his mind about Neo-Gers being a new team, he had previously accused Stephen Thompson, chairman of Dundee United, of leaking stories about the SPL to the press. He made this sound like the most heinous of crimes.[4] Now it seemed like he was doing the same thing. It was also rather hypocritical that he was leaking stories to the anti-Green faction when it was Green that had given him his well-paid sinecure.

At the start of August Leggat almost had apoplexy when Charles Green returned to Ibrox. He had been brought in as a consultant to 'promote the interests of Rangers Football Club, specifically assisting with shareholder relations and advising the company on its capital structure,' as the club statement said.[5] Bill McMurdo was, understandably, overjoyed.

It has to be said that this was a remarkable move by the board. Among all the demonstrations against spivs and crooks, Green's name was uppermost. Aside from Bill McMurdo and his followers, Green's name was reviled and hated almost as much as that of Whyte. He was accused of using his 'big Yorkshire hands' to scoop up all the money that had come into Neo-Gers and his French chateau was a major bone of contention. How the hell he was going to do anything for shareholder relations was a mystery. Either the board was seriously detached from the zeitgeist among the club's support or they simply didn't give a fuck. Either that or they just did it to piss Walter Smith off.

It was only a couple of days after Green's appointment that the resignation of Walter Smith was announced. Apparently he had been opposed to Green coming back (surprise, surprise) but was voted down by the rest of the board. Feeling that his position was untenable, he left.[6] Of course, he couldn't go quietly and made sure he had a little dig at the board in his statement to the press. He called

89

for change in the boardroom and it was obvious that he was backing those shareholders trying to get rid of Green.[7]

Malcolm Murray had done exactly the same thing when he left, moaning about the need for transparency and integrity. He also told of how he had had to pay an Ibrox electricity bill with his own money! He invoked the ghost of Bill Struth, saying that he would be spinning in his grave at everything that had been happening.[8] Murray wasn't the first to bring up the name of the Arthur Askey look-a-like and he certainly wouldn't be the last.

Charlie Boy, meanwhile, wasn't exactly making himself any friends on his return. He said that if Sooperally didn't win a cup this year then he had a problem.[9] This reminded everyone of what he had said earlier in the year, when he had played the Comic Book Guy in the Simpsons and called Sooperally's team the worst 'Rangers' team ever.[10] No wonder he was becoming such a hate figure. Well, to everyone except Bill McMurdo.

The whole thing was turning into a war. On the one side was Green, the Easdales, Brian Stockbridge and Craig Mather, the CEO. On the other side was Jim McColl (not the Beechgrove Garden one but another of the Daily Record's billionaires), Paul Murray, a member of David Murray's old board, Malcolm Murray, who we already know, and two guys called Alex Wilson and Scott Murdoch. The latter bunch was trying to get onto the board and had called, or requisitioned, an EGM for this purpose; hence the name they were called, The Requisitioners.

The Requisitioners appeared to anyone on the outside as just a bunch of disgruntled troublemakers, desperately trying to climb aboard the gravy train. Amazingly, however, such was their hatred of the Neo-Gers board that many of The People were prepared to follow follow these clowns. They gathered outside Ibrox chanting, they waved their pish-stained bedsheets and their maws' good tablecloths about and shouted anti-board slogans at every match.

The Daily Record nailed its colours firmly to the mast. On the day that Smith 'walked away' they printed his full statement. They also printed a joint statement from the Rangers Supporters Association, Rangers Supporters Assembly and the Rangers Supporters Trust, who all expressed their distrust of the board and called for them to accede to the EGM demands. The Record even wheeled out Donald

Findlay, of all people, to give his take on things. He spoke of the current battles as being 'not the Rangers way' and said that in his day 'we conducted ourselves in a certain manner,' doing 'everything behind closed doors where everything was secretive.'[11] So much for Malcolm Murray's call for transparency!

As far as the blogs went it was Bill McMurdo against all the others. Not only Leggat was on the side of The Requisitioners but Follow Follow and all the rest, apart from Vanguard Bears, who were biding their time to see how things were going to turn out. The hatred and bile that poured out on these blogs was incredible, especially when you realised that it was The People versus The People.

All of us normal people (with a small 'p') didn't have a side to take in this war; both sides were as bad and as mental as each other. Besides, nobody was interested in what we thought; we were 'Rangers-haters'! These were the only things that The People could actually agree on: hatred of everybody else and holding firm to the Big Lie.

Of course, they knew, deep in their hearts, that Rangers had died but they couldn't bear to see or hear anyone confirm it. McMurdo banned anyone that made such a statement on his blog, while others resorted to a rather ridiculous tit-for-tat affair. This childish argument was that Celtic had changed its name in 1994 so was a 'new club'. They also said that McCann had set up some company called Pacific Shelf to buy Celtic so they started to call Celtic 'Pacific Shelf'. This, of course, was nonsense.

Who remembers the chocolate bar Marathon? In 1990 the name was changed to Snickers, to fall into line with what it was called everywhere else in the world. Other products did the same: Oil of Ulay became Oil of Olay and Jif became Cif. There could be no argument whatsoever that they were the same products, just with a different name.

A different story entirely was the magazine Punch. Anybody that's done History at school is bound to have come across at least one cartoon from this organ. It was started in 1841 and was extremely popular among the middle and upper classes and even royalty. After 151 years of unbroken history the magazine folded and ceased publication in 1992.

In 1996 Mohamed Al-Fayed bought the rights to the name and

began publishing his own version of Punch. Even though it had the same name, nobody thought of this as the same magazine or in any way a continuation of the old one. The old Punch had died; this was a completely new Punch.

That's what The People couldn't get their heads round; a change of name means nothing, while the death of a product means that a subsequent re-incarnation is, by its very nature, a new product entirely. Celtic never went into liquidation; Rangers, on the contrary, did.

They were also making a huge mistake in logic. A basic rule of logic is that you can't make inferences based on a fallacy: for example, If A means that B is true, it doesn't necessarily follow that B causes A to be true and vice-versa. If Celtic became a new club in 1994 then that means, necessarily, that Green's club was a new one. That is a true statement. You can't, however, turn it round, like you can with a sum or product equation and say that if Green's club was a new one
then that means Celtic became a new club in 1994. Logic doesn't work like that; unless, of course, you happen to be pretty dense.

Still, that didn't stop The People getting riled whenever somebody pointed out that they were following a new club. It's a bit like the way children can get angry at school. Children being children, they like nothing better than to annoy one another, especially if they can get some sort of reaction. They'll whisper things like, 'Your maw's a cow!' or 'You're da's a an auld jakey!' or 'Your maw's a junkie!' Usually the other kids will answer in kind or challenge them, saying, 'What ye sayin', ya wee dobber!' I've seen one or two children, however, that completely lost the plot when somebody said such things to them. Books and jotters were thrown everywhere and chairs and desks were kicked over. (Of course, muggins here had to tidy it all up!) One lad threw an electric pencil sharpener through a window!

I soon discovered the reason for this extreme reaction: the childrens' mothers *were* junkies! This provides an excellent explanation for the reactions of The People when you tell them their team's dead: they know fine well that it is!

16
Garageland

A way back when I was training to be a primary-school teacher, I had to learn about nursery children as well. Many primary schools have nurseries within them and, as a teacher, you are expected to be able (but hopefully never asked) to run a nursery. Nurseries these days aren't just about reading nursery rhymes and wiping snotters. There's actually a curriculum and you're expected to teach the children certain things. Of course, the pished pants and runny noses are still there, which is why there aren't many teachers queuing up for the job. But you still have to learn about it.

One of the things we learned was to look out for signs of maturity; that a child was ready to move on to school. I argued that if one of these signs was a sign of immaturity then there was a hell of a lot of immature adults walking about!

The sign of maturity that we read about was in a book about child psychology. The psychologist offered the children in a nursery a bar of chocolate but they could have two bars of chocolate if they were prepared to wait until later. Most of the children just grabbed the one bar, only thinking of the here-and-now, while a few were willing to wait. This, apparently, was a sign of how mature those few were.

How many adults are prepared to wait for things? And is there anything wrong with not waiting? Some Spartan, usually middle-class, souls see debt as something to be avoided at all costs, even if you are going without in the process. I remember one teacher driving a beaten-up old car into school, saying that she and her husband were still saving for a new one. They had saved three years to get him one and now they were saving for hers. When I suggested HP she nearly had a heart attack; debt was bad. She went in the huff when I asked if they were saving up for twenty-five years to buy a house; apparently a mortgage doesn't count as debt.

I certainly don't see any difference between taking out a mortgage and taking on a bank loan, or some other kind of finance, to purchase something you either need or want right at this minute.

And there are plenty of folk out there that obviously agree with me.

What the hell has this got to do with anything? Well, remember the 1990s when Rangers were running away with everything? Fergus McCann came in and started building for the future. None of the supporters were too happy about this; all that they could see was that Rangers were closing in on Celtic's nine-in-a-row record and The Bunnet wouldn't spend enough money to stop them. In hindsight it's easy to see that he did the right thing but at the time it was sore to take.

Now think of the Rangers supporters. Their club had died but now everyone was telling them that it hadn't. It was the same team with its world record of fifty-four titles. What do you think their main worry was going to be? Exactly the same as that of the Celtic supporters in the nineties: they were terrified that they might be stuck down in the bottom tiers for years on end while Celtic won title after title and overtook their record. Remember the hurt and anger when Rangers equaled Celtic's record in 1997? You can imagine, then, how The People felt.

Perhaps if everyone had accepted that Rangers had died, instead of promoting the Big Lie, then The People might have been able to deal with their grief and support their new team's progress up the leagues. Moving on is part of the process, after all. Instead, they were fed the story that Rangers was still around and the 'biggest team in Scotland.' It was hardly surprising, then, that they demanded immediate success.

It was expected in all quarters that Neo-Gers, or Rangers as they all insisted on calling it, would storm its way up through the leagues. They were in the fourth tier so it would take three years to get 'back' into the SPL, then another year to win that and then it was on into Europe. They all honestly believed this, both the support and our Fourth Estate. It was going to be that easy.

Who had time to bring youngsters up through the ranks? The transfer embargo didn't kick in until September so Sooperally had time to shop around and see what he could get. He had no money for transfer fees but he managed to get a few folk and he still had one or two that hadn't buggered off, like Lee McCulloch. (Who else would have him?) It was going to cost a hefty sum in wages but if that was what was needed then so be it. Critics might go on about sledgehammers and nuts but winning Division 3 was an absolute must. Cutting cloth was for wimps!

The 2012-13 season was agony for The People. Sooperally's team was so bad that it was hard to tell sometimes during a match which were the professionals and which were the amateurs. Getting pumped out of the Scottish Cup by Dundee United and the League Cup by Inverness were sore ones but the defeat to Queen of the South in the Ramsden's Cup almost had The People tearing their hair out in despair. Eventually, however, Neo-Gers, as expected, won Division 3, with some of the more deluded claiming it as title number 55!

There were a few grumbles about the money being spent and Charles Green's golden handshake nearly caused uproar. All-in-all, though, it was felt that big money had to be spent: after all, this was 'Rangers'! As 2013 went on, however, the grumbling got louder and louder as details started to leak out about where the money was going. It was beginning to look as if Neo-Gers was just a gravy train for those in the boardroom.

Despite these grumbles, it was still widely held that this club was still Rangers, a world-class club, the 'biggest club in Scotland' and on a par with the likes of Barcelona and Manchester United, even if they were playing in the bottom tiers. When a new team bus was unveiled in June, therefore, none of The People raised an eyebrow; it was no more than a top-class club like 'Rangers' deserved.

The rest of us laughed at this vanity project, supplied by Bruce's bus company. The vehicle had Wi-Fi, a separate sleeping section, facilities for a physio, satellite TV, a Playstation 3, a fridge, an oven and hotplate, an onboard swimming pool, casino, practice pitch, hotel with function suite and a fully-staffed bordello at the back. It was 'inspired' by Liverpool FC's luxury coach, which that team used to travel to all games in Europe.[1] The Neo-Gers coach's first trip was going to be to the exotic village of Brora for a pre-season match against the local team!

The coach could also be hired for corporate meetings and functions. Fortunately, the bus was fitted with extra-wide seats because, as we all know, the arses of the Govan bears are bigger than the average bear's! Half-a-million quid this monstrosity cost so, hopefully, Bruce's were going to be inundated with booking requests.

Unlike the Liverpool bus, the Neo-Gers coach never got the chance to travel on the wrong side of the road or even to experience the delights of a gang of The People out on a stag night. A few weeks after it being unveiled the bus went up in flames. Not only that but the old coach was parked next to it and it went to bus heaven as well. I believe the Neo-Gers players were issued with bus passes for the coming season.

A hole had been cut through a perimeter fence and the lock on the garage door forced. A police spokesman said that it was apparent that the fire had been started deliberately. Police Scotland revealed that the blaze was being treated as 'suspicious'.[2] (Aye, there's no flies on our boys in blue, eh?)

The immediate reaction of The People was that some 'Fenian bastard' had done the deed out of envy. As more details emerged, however, especially the fact that there were gas cylinders on-site, it seemed like there might be a more sinister explanation. Was it an insurance job? Or was it the work of some rival bus company? Maybe it's better not to go down that particular path.

Rumours had been doing the rounds for months that Neo-Gers were operating with losses of £1m a month. The Neo-Gers bloggers of course, denied this, calling it scare stories by 'Rangers-haters'. Some of The People, however, weren't so sure. The club itself hardly allayed any of these fears by not publishing accounts. In fact, no accounts had emanated from Ibrox since 2011. Comforting noises came from the boardroom about there not being a crisis and there being plenty of money.

Such was the split in the Neo-Gers support that some would not believe anything the board said on point of principle; others argued that the anti-board faction was making up figures, aided and abetted by 'Rangers-haters'. And then we discovered Sooperally's salary.

£825,000 a year was a wage that even some English Premiership managers would envy. It was the largest football salary in Scotland; twice what Neil Lennon was getting. Did he deserve such a huge remuneration package, especially considering that his team was so shite? After all, they were knocked out of the first round of the League Cup by Forfar, weren't they? Still, this was 'Rangers' we were talking about, the biggest club in Scotland. Amazingly, more than a few were actually proud of Sooperally's huge wage packet, seeing it as a sign of how financially secure Neo-Gers were. Sooperally himself was understandably embarrassed and promised to take a reduction in salary post-haste.

The accounts were published at the start of October and showed the finances of Neo-Gers for a thirteen-month period up to June 30th. It showed that the rumours had been right; operating losses were shown to be £14.4m for the period. This tied in completely with what everybody had been saying about the club hemorrhaging £1m a month. Surely even the most diehard supporter of the board had to see that there was something wrong?

Incredibly there were still those that argued that things weren't that bad. McMurdo saw positives but conceded that cuts would have to be made.[3] Kieran Prior, a Neo-Gers shareholder with an 'off-the-radar' IQ, who had been a trader at Goldman-Sachs, said that the loss was not the board's fault. He said that even Bill Gates would have struggled to make a profit at Ibrox and that most of the expenditure had
been on one-off items. He declared that he considered his investment safe.[4]

All the payments outlined in the accounts were grist to the mill of The Requisitioners. It looked like Neo-Gers was just one big gravy train, with those at the top taking far more than the players. Green had gone before the accounts were published, being sacked in the middle of August, which was just as well as he'd managed to get his big mitts on nearly a million quid just in salary and bonuses. Brian Stockbridge was due a massive bonus for Neo-Gers winning Division 3; a bonus of £200,000 to be exact. This threw the anti-board faction into a frenzy. There was no Green or Ahmad around anymore so Stockbridge became the focus of The People's ire.

Leggat, of course, now turned on the last of his Three Musketeers.[5] Green, Ahmad and Stockbridge were now akin to the Second Triumvirate from Shakespeare's Julius Caesar, callously carving up everything between them. The case of The Requisitioners seemed stronger than ever.

17
Deny

The members of the Scottish media had got themselves excited during 2013. With Walter Smith installed as chairman and rumours that Dave King was coming back, they could almost taste that roast lamb. Sadly, this tantalising prospect was cruelly dashed when King failed to come up with the goods and Smith resigned. Who was going to supply that succulent taste of best New Zealand now? The ones ensconced on the board at present were not keen at all on the old style of doing things, which annoyed our Fourth Estate no end.

The media kept up their part, selling the Big Lie as best they could. By the second half of 2013 they had even gone as far as eliminating the 'L' word altogether. The only thing ever mentioned was administration, making it seem as if Green's CVA had been accepted. Scratch that. Green was no longer a part of the story; the tale now was that the supporters had saved 'Rangers'. It was as if our media took what had happened at Celtic in 1994 and grafted it onto the story of Rangers.

Even the BBC joined in. Instead of being liquidated, Rangers were now described as having 'experienced a major insolvency event'.[1] I suppose they were right; you can't get much more of a major insolvency event than liquidation!

All this denial, however, meant nothing if the club the media were touting as Rangers didn't act like Rangers; where was the cosy relationship? Where were the press handouts? And, more importantly, where the hell were the lamb dinners? No wonder the press wanted the Easdales ousted and the old guard installed back in the Blue Room.

There was major excitement when it seemed, in October, that Dave King was on his way back yet again. He held talks with Craig Mather, the CEO, and Brian Stockbridge, about pumping funds into Neo-Gers. His price was that he would be installed as chairman and that there would be a new shares issue.[2] If this could be achieved, then Mather and Stockbridge might trump The Requisitioners at the upcoming AGM.

In order to clear the way for King's return, our press had to resort to more bending of the truth. We were told that King had 'settled' his tax dispute with the South African authorities.[3] He had agreed on a 'settlement' of £43.7m, allowing criminal charges against him to be dropped.[4] So now everything was above board and nobody could object to King becoming chairman of a company. The reality, however, was somewhat different.

South African media reported that, as well as the 'settlement' figure, King actually pleaded guilty to contravening the SA Income Tax Act. He had to pay a fine of 208 million Rand (nearly £12m) or face two years in prison.[5] Strangely, no mention of this was made in our media.

What was discussed in our media was whether or not King would pass as a 'fit and proper person' by the regulations of both the Stock Exchange and the SFA. The Daily Record went out on a limb and declared that a Stock Exchange 'spokesman' had said that King would be passed by the Stock Exchange with no problems.[6] Now all he had to worry about was the SFA.

Although the SFA has no 'fit and proper person' test per se, it still has the power under its rules to block the appointment of an individual to a club board, with the club facing losing its licence if it doesn't comply. Hugh Keevins did the usual Daily Record trick of trying to get everybody worked up by pointing out that Peter Lawwell would have a say in vetting King. Keevins went further, suggesting that Lawwell 'may' have the 'casting vote,' in other words, he would get to make the decision.[7] Lawell himself, however, soon knocked this story on the head, saying that he would probably absent himself in such circumstances.[8]

As far as The People were concerned, the SFA could mind its own business. Who were they to decide who was fit or not? A 'cabal' run by Peter Lawell for the good of Celtic; that's all the SFA was. Remarkably, The People blamed the SFA for all Rangers' troubles because they hadn't blocked Craig Whyte's takeover. If they had tried you can bet The People would have reacted in exactly the same way as they were doing now.

Meanwhile, The Requisitioners had managed to get a court ruling to postpone the AGM until December. This would mean that the board would have to put The Requisitioners' proposals to the shareholders, as well as giving twenty-one days' notice of when, exactly, the AGM would take place.

Neo-Gers had also shed more personnel. Craig Mather, the CEO, and Bryan Smart, a non-executive director, both resigned in the middle of October. Mather claimed that he was leaving for the good of the club but to outsiders it looked like rats deserting a sinking ship. Of course, Mather was entitled to a year's salary and walked off with £300,000,[9] a fact that enraged

The Requisitioners. In a statement to the Stock Exchange, Neo-Gers thanked both men for their contributions to the club.

No such thanks for somebody else that left at the start of November. All that was said on the Neo-Gers website was, 'Rangers today announce that Director of Communications James Traynor has left the Club.' He could hardly have expected more; in his ten months at the club he achieved the sum total of bugger all. A few statements on the website, lashing out at everyone with toothless threats was all he appeared to have done.

In the latter half of 2013 newspaper photographs usually showed him skulking about in the background in the director's box. The rumours about him feeding stories to Leggat probably didn't exactly help his case for being kept on. The story that came out of Ibrox was that he had left as part of cost-cutting measures. He promptly disappeared without a trace, probably crying his eyes out somewhere.

Also doing a disappearing act was Dave King, which made all the 'fit and proper person' arguments redundant. After stocking up on mint sauce, our media men had to face up to another disappointment. King said that he had spoken to both sides of the boardroom battle and felt that they both had a case. Everyone was far too intransigent, however, to even think of making compromises. He predicted that there would be an 'acrimonious' AGM and that the meeting would be 'indecisive'.[10] It didn't need a crystal ball to predict that; all you needed to do was read the Neo
Gers blogs and websites to know that no quarter was going to be given.

The only hope of a return to the good old days now lay with The Requisitioners. One of them was Paul Murray, who used to be on David Murray's board. Surely his farts would smell of roast lamb just as much as King's?

18
Remote Control

There's nothing folk like better than a good conspiracy theory. Whether it be Area 51, Skull and Bones or the New World Order, everybody likes finding out that there's somebody up there pulling the strings. Why people want to believe all this stuff I don't know; it's hardly going to make you sleep any easier at night, is it?

If there's nothing there then people feel the need to invent it. The Priory of Sion, the Rosicrucians and the Illuminati are just some of the secret societies that folk have invented to give them nightmares. Even governments get in on the act, scaring us all shitless with tales of sophisticated cave systems in Afghanistan, where an international terrorist group called Al Qaeda meets to make plans to murder us all in our beds. Even when it's proven that these caves don't exist and neither does Al Qaeda it doesn't stop folk from believing every word.

And then we have the real organisations that everybody likes to think are mixed up in big, secret conspiracies. Folk in the Orange Order would have you believe that the Jesuits are just such an organisation. There are whole websites devoted to this pish. There are also places on the internet where you can read the same garbage about Freemasons, who are really just groups of men dressing up, mumbling things about Great Architects or whatever and then getting pissed.

Then there's the lunatic fringe, the completely out-there folk that seem to have got their ideas from watching the X-Files. The Royals are all reptilian aliens, the late Queen Mother was a practising Satanist and child murderer, we are all under some mind-control project and the Jews are running the world for some nefarious purpose. There was even one bam that wrote a book called Torrent about a conspiracy in Scotland!

We've already looked at the paranoia of The People and their contention that there had been some big conspiracy against their old and new clubs. But they went even further than that. It wasn't just a conspiracy against 'Rangers'; it was a conspiracy against what they called the Protestant, Unionist, Loyalist community.

In essence, the PUL community is simply another, euphemistic, name for the Orange Order. Certainly there are many that hate this organisation, and with good reason, but to the majority of people it is an anachronistic embarrassment. Orange parades belong in a bygone age of pogroms against Jews and the lynching of black people; it has no place in a modern, civilised society. There's been no deliberate campaign against this organisation; it's just dying a natural death. Most Scottish people can't see the point and view the Orange Order not as a positive thing but a negative one, filled with hatred.

Go on any website dedicated to 'Rangers' and you'll find a lot of bleating about the PUL community being under threat. Follow any links on the website and you'll find more of the same. Like the EDL and the BNP they think their 'traditions' and 'culture' are under threat. What these 'traditions' and 'culture' are they seem unwilling to point out. If they want to follow the Protestant faith and support the Royal family, then nobody's stopping them; in fact, there are many that do so without banging a drum or blowing a flute. Nobody's destroying their culture; it's just that the rest of us are moving on and leaving them behind.

It's the same anywhere you get some old, right-wing organisation that no longer has a place in society. The Ku Klux Klan have become pretty much an irrelevance and they, of course, blame outside forces for their decline. The same can be said for the South African organisation, the AWB, whose views no longer reflect those of the majority of whites there. The Orange Order in Scotland is in the same, invidious position; most people don't care anymore about others' religious beliefs and feel nothing but embarrassment at racial hatred of the Irish. Meanwhile, just like their counterparts abroad, the members of the Orange Order blame everyone else for their decline.

Like a dinosaur in its death throes they lash about at all and sundry. Britannia no longer rules the waves and they are no longer the master race and this is difficult to accept. Instead of facing reality they desperately cling to the past and see the changing world as a conspiracy to knock them off their imagined pedestal.

For many years now, all their hopes and dreams had been wrapped up in their football team, Rangers; in fact, the Orange Order actually once owned shares in Rangers FC.[1] Their feelings of superiority were expressed through their football club; dominating Scottish football, world records, five-star stadium and all the rest of the things they bragged about. Now it had all been cruelly taken away; their last bastion of superiority gone. No wonder they were so desperate to cling to the Big Lie!

But the Big Lie wasn't enough; they knew it wasn't Rangers and so did the rest of us. What they needed to make the Big Lie more robust was to have 'Real Rangers Men' in charge; then they could pretend that all was well with the world. After all, their whole raison d'être was based on a fantasy; one more couldn't hurt.

Right from the start Green had his work cut out trying to convince everybody that he was the right man. He did his best by calling all the other clubs in Scotland 'bigots' and constantly spouting all manner of nonsense about conspiracies against his club. His sucking up to The People even extended to going to Belfast to rouse the troops there. He also went to Australia and America to speak to supporters groups and promote the idea of 'Rangers' as a global brand. Try as he might, however, there was still a groundswell of opinion against him.

The attempt by Walter Smith and his cronies to get rid of him showed how precarious his position was. Even Jabba wasn't totally convinced. He obviously agreed with all Green's bluster and blame but he said that Green had better deliver. 'Rangers fans have given him their trust and a further misuse of that belief would be the biggest abuse of all,' he said.[2] A little warning there that Green had better watch his step.

The major concern expressed about Green was about his backers. Who were Margarita Holdings and Blue Pitch Holdings? Why were they so secretive about their identities? It's not as if secrecy wasn't the 'Rangers Way' but there are secrets and there are secrets. In the good old days, meetings at Ibrox might be top secret and nobody knew what was going on in the Blue Room unless David Murray sanctioned it. At least, however, everybody knew *who* was running the show.

Secrecy always gives rise to speculation and speculation was, of course, rife as to who was behind these shady organisations. The name on most lips was that of Craig Whyte; could it be possible that Beelzebub was still behind the scenes, running everything? The thought gave The People nightmares and prompted that little voice nagging in the back of their minds that 'Real Rangers Men' should be in charge.

Even more worrying were some of the extreme possibilities. Maybe Russian gangsters had control of Neo-Gers. Or worse, perhaps the Vatican Bank was behind one of these shadowy companies. Most disconcerting of all was the thought that Dermot Desmond could be involved somewhere. The People would rather the Queen became a Catholic or the Pope was elected Moderator of the General Assembly of the Church of Scotland than have that happen!

Just as many of The People are convinced that descendants of Irish immigrants have infiltrated councils, the Scottish and Westminster Governments and the Civil Service in order to destroy the 'traditions' of the 'PUL Community', so the idea of a conspiracy was easily transferred to the owners of the Ibrox club. What if there had been infiltration there as well? Who knew what nefarious plans they were hatching, or even implementing? No wonder The People wanted 'Real Rangers Men' in charge.

In August 2012 the BBC revealed that the man behind Blue Pitch Holdings was somebody called Arif Naqvi from Dubai.[3] Well, he seemed harmless enough so why the need for all the secrecy? The guy was, more likely than not, a Muslim so maybe he thought The People wouldn't like that. But, unless Muslims had suddenly started making the Sign of the Cross, he would have had no worries on that score!

This was the only mention I could find anywhere of this guy being involved in Blue Pitch Holdings so it remains to be seen if the BBC report is true or not. Green himself denied it. It certainly didn't put anyone's mind at rest.

John 'Bomber' Brown had raised concerns right at the start of Green's tenure. He was the guy in the ill-fitting suit that demanded to see the deeds. Nobody really paid any attention to him at first but his words stuck in the minds of The People and the agnivores. It was a constant reminder that there were no longer 'Rangers Men' in

104

charge at Ibrox. Not only that but it was actually unclear who, exactly, *was* in charge.

This lack of transparency presented those that supported the current regime with a huge dilemma. Yes, Green had 'saved Rangers' and appeared to be looking to the future, bringing in worldwide investors, even if everyone was unsure who these investors were. But, on the other hand, the PUL Community was under attack on all sides, especially from those seeking Scottish independence. Was Neo-Gers to be just another football team, or a leading light in the war against independence seekers, Catholicisers, anti-monarchist elements, Irish Republicans and other assorted ne'erdowells? Bill McMurdo probably needed a dozen valium tablets just to get to sleep at night!

19
Hitsville UK

Bill McMurdo was Green's biggest supporter. He wasn't too slavish about it and pulled him up for some of his more outlandish outpourings but, as far as McMurdo was concerned, Green was the right man in the right place. Everybody agreed with him, or seemed to agree with him, at first; even Leggat was fulsome in his praise of Green. But, as the plot to get rid of Green right at the start had shown, it couldn't last.

As the cries mounted to get rid of Green it seemed that McMurdo was the only one on his side. But, then, he had his band of followers that posted on his blog. All of them agreed that Green and his board were the good guys and they had to fight against the 'rebels'.

To the outsider it was hard to figure out who was in the majority in the big struggle to control Ibrox. It was hard enough normally to figure out what constituted a majority of The People, as 40,000 of them singing The Billy Boys was usually referred to as a 'small minority'! But how many were backing Green and how many wanted rid of him?

The problem with The People is that they are great lovers of hyperbole. Not for them just calling a local supporters group the Auchtermuchty Rangers Supporters Group or whatever; it's got to be the Auchtermuchty International Loyal Apprentice 1690 Derry Boys or some such, even though there are only four of them in a car going to matches together. There are so many of these mobs that it's hard to keep track and to know how many supporters each group represents.

The anti-board mob was certainly louder; shouting and waving their stained bedsheets in the Broomloan Stand. McMurdo, however, made an equal claim to represent the majority. The millions of hits he boasts that his blog receives[1] are impressive; even though the same people make multiple posts every day, so obviously they made multiple visits. But, still, a million is a bloody big number by any standard.

Anyway, whoever had the majority on their side, it became clear as 2013 progressed that the Neo-Gers support was split, seemingly irrevocably. McMurdo professed to be against the brown-brogue-wearing 'Real Rangers Men' and to be all in favour of a new, forward-looking 'Rangers'. But is that what he really wanted? Despite his and his supporters' hatred of the 'rebels' many of the things he said would inspire any 'Real Rangers Man'.

In December 2012 McMurdo was beating the drum for the Ulster Loyalists and their fight to keep the Union Flag flying constantly over Belfast City Hall.[2] He and they saw it as some kind of big Republican conspiracy. In reality it was just bringing Belfast into line with every other city in the UK, where the Union Flag was only flown on special occasions. It was a choice between Belfast being a normal, UK city and an outpost of empire. It was obvious which one the Loyalists wanted.

McMurdo said that he was going to be at the demonstration in George Square to make a stand for Unionism and expected many from the 'Rangers family' to be there. After all, as he put it, 'Rangers is traditionally a Unionist club supported by those loyal to the Throne and the Union in Scotland.'[3] So to McMurdo, and to many others, Rangers, and Neo-Gers, were much, much more than a football team. That was why everybody had it in for them.

Now that sounded like a clarion call for 'Real Rangers Men' in the Blue Room and, arguably, that's how many of his readers would take it. Not all of McMurdo's readership agreed with his support for the board, pre- and post-Green. You could tell this from some of the posts but, as the split became more intense and the arguments became more heated, McMurdo banned such dissenting voices from his blog. The fact that he had to do so shows that there were those reading his blog that wanted rid of the board.

And why wouldn't they? As McMurdo himself argued, the Ibrox club was more than just a football team; it stood for a lot more than that. Would Green, Ahmad, the Easdales, Blue Pitch Holdings, Margarita Holdings and the rest give a gorilla's wank about flags in Belfast? Most likely not, so it was essential to get folk onto the board that understood the 'traditions' associated with what they were still calling 'Rangers'.

As McMurdo has said many times on his blog, Unionism and

Loyalism mean far more to him than the Ibrox club; the fight to keep Scotland as part of the UK was far more important than the fight to save 'Rangers'. Keeping the United Kingdom together was all part-and-parcel of his mystical vision for Britain, gleaned from all the pseudo-histories that had sprung up in Victorian times to justify Britain's dominance in the world. Britain was no longer a dominant force but that didn't stop the likes of McMurdo from still believing in the idea of destiny in these fairy tales.

The fear of Scottish independence went far deeper than that for The People; it went to the heart of their beliefs. English people couldn't give a stuff about Northern Ireland and see both sides as being as bad as each other. They'd like the whole area to just disappear. The Ulster Unionists rely on their connection with Scotland to maintain a link with the United Kingdom and the monarchy. If Scotland were to leave the UK, where would that leave them? This was the great terror of the Loyalists in Northern Ireland and it was transmuted to their supporters in Scotland.

Of course, none of them could express their fear in these terms; it might actually jeopardise the 'No' vote to be so explicit. And so, as usual, they couched their concerns in language that suggested a grand conspiracy. It was Republicans, with a capital 'r' that were to blame, trying to turn Scotland into some version of the Irish Republic. The People, including McMurdo, even went so far as to claim that Alex Salmond had long been an associate of Irish Republicans!

Amazingly, McMurdo also accused those that wanted Scottish independence of racism. 'Racial hatred of the English drives the independence campaign,'[4] he stated. Quite where he got this from I've no idea since it was the 'No' camp that traded in scare stories and personality assassination, not those for independence. If anything the pro-independence side was against being ruled from Westminster, something that many English people could equally relate to. His playing of the race card was disingenuous to say the least.

Anti-Irish racism is something that has gone on in our country, both Scotland and the UK, for a long, long time. It has become so ingrained that people don't even notice it any more. I once went to an SFA training day for those coaching children. I was soon coughing my lungs up and was considering a trip to the A & E as we had to take part in the activities that were suggested for training children. One of the ideas we were given was to use silly forfeits for folk that got something wrong or that came last. This was intended to make football training more of a fun activity than it had been in the past. Being over forty and unfit, I, of course, had to do a few of these forfeits, which, if you're involved in football coaching, you'll be familiar with.

One of these forfeits involved lying on your back and shoving your hands up and down with flat palms, as if you were doing press-ups the wrong way round. The coach called these 'Irish press-ups.' The thought behind this is that a whole race of people is thick. Not racist? What if he had made a joke about Jews being stingy or Arabs being suicide bombers?

The thing is that many of us grew up with casual racism and accepted it as an everyday occurrence. When I was a boy we thought nothing of going to the local grocer's shop and asking for a pound of 'darkies' sausages' when we were sent to buy black pudding. Everybody thought this kind of 'banter' was hilarious and saw no harm in it. With hindsight it's completely cringe-worthy and by the time I was seventeen I wouldn't have dreamt of saying such a thing.

It's the same with every area of society. Celtic fans threw bananas at Mark Walters when he was playing for Rangers back in the 1980s. They weren't the only ones indulging in racist behaviour, although The People would have you believe they were. Times have moved on and folk have grown up. It would be a brave man that would indulge in such activities at Celtic Park these days; he'd be banned for life and probably end up on the wrong end of a kicking.

Racism against the Irish, however, is the last bastion of this kind of chauvinism. Like the racism against black people thirty or forty years ago, it's dismissed as 'just banter' and those that complain about it have no sense of humour. Mention the word 'Hun,' though and you'll be accused of all manner of bigotry!

McMurdo took the line that anti-Irish racism did not, indeed could not, exist. He argued that the Scots and the Irish were essentially the same race and that 'you cannot be racist against your own race'.[5] Really? So all those black comedians that were around in the 60s and 70s, pandering to their white audiences by demeaning themselves and their race weren't being racist? And what about the English?

109

You can't just leave them out of the melting pot.

The British Isles have been invaded so many times by Romans, Northumbrians, Angles, Saxons, Vikings and Normans to name but a few and there have been so many comings-and-goings among these islands as well as between here and the continent that you'd be hard-pushed to find a purely indigenous Scotsman, Irishman, Welshman or Englishman. This goes some way to supporting McMurdo's contention that we're all one race, although it certainly doesn't excuse anti-Irish sentiments. It also, however, proves that his talk of 'anti-English racism,' by his own logic, is nothing but pish!

Anyway, to McMurdo Scottish nationalism was the driving force behind the big conspiracy against 'Rangers'. 'Rangers as a force for Unionism is a frightening prospect for separatists so how convenient for them that the support base is crippled by splits and divisions at this crucial time.'[6] In fact, he was convinced that it was more than mere convenience. 'Those who think it merely circumstantial that a club traditionally known as a bastion of Unionism should find itself crippled by divisions and splits at a time when the Union needs it most have a stronger belief in coincidence than I do.'[7] He even said that part of his reason for opposing the 'Requisitioner' Jim McColl was because he was for Scottish independence.[8]

Notwithstanding this opposition to McColl it was hard to argue that the current members of the Neo-Gers board were great supporters of the Union. As long as it didn't impact on their pockets then we could vote for a Fascist or Communist dictatorship or to become part of France for all they cared. Anyone taking McMurdo's views to heart, therefore, would again see the need for 'Real Rangers Men' to be in place. McMurdo's arguments appeared to be making the case for the ones he professed to be opposing.

20
Last Gang in Town

The Rangers Supporters Assembly, The Rangers Supporters Trust, Vanguard Bears, The Union Bears, The Blue Order and, my favourite, The Rangers Worldwide Alliance. For every Rangers, or Neo-Gers, supporter there seems to be a supporters' group. You can just imagine a meeting of The Rangers Worldwide Alliance: old Billy McWilliams, the sole member, sipping at a pint down the Louden. Every June, The Rangers Worldwide Alliance has its annual social evening, when old Billy takes his wife with him.

With so many supporters groups it was difficult to present any kind of united front. They could hardly say that all the supporters were against the board when it was obvious that there were those that still supported it. What they needed was some name that conjured up old Rangers and the old days. There was only one character that epitomised everything that Rangers had stood for; that sense of superiority, that sense of destiny and that good, old-fashioned bigotry. That name was Struth; the name of the man that had made Rangers what it was. And so the Sons of Struth were born.

Bill Struth was probably turning in his grave when he saw all the pishy bedsheets and bath towels being brandished in his name. Whatever else might be said about Struth, there's no denying that he was always well turned-out and dapper. He also, however, had an exaggerated sense of his own importance; a trait shared with all of those currently taking his name in vain.

Their Facebook page described the Sons of Struth as 'A body of like minded Rangers fans who hold dear the values of Struth. Dignity, honesty and openness.'[1] These are the kinds of words you always hear associated with Struth, especially in the hagiographies written about him. The way they go on it makes it sound as if Jesus wasn't worthy of cleaning Struth's boots. So what was the truth?

The reality is that Struth was one of those characters that was so private that it's virtually impossible to discover a lot about him.

Much of what has been written about him tends to rely on anecdotal evidence, which is completely unreliable. Stories of showing doomed Canadians around the stadium in the middle of the night, looking after runaway canaries and accompanying injured players to hospital paint a picture of a saintly man.[2] This is quite a feat, considering the question marks that hang about the man's character.

Struth was the architect, along with the Rangers chairman, John Ure Primrose, of the long-standing, sectarian signing policy at Ibrox. Then there was the mysterious disappearance of Struth's boss, Rangers manager, William Wilton, when the two of them went out fishing on a boat off Gourock. There was also Struth's disgraceful treatment of Sam English.

This young man suffered serious psychological problems after the accidental death of Johnny Thompson and, arguably, never recovered. Anyone in his position should have had time out and a course of therapy. Arguing that such psychological conditions were misunderstood in the 1930s in nonsense. Treatment of mental illness had come along way since quivering wrecks, suffering from PTSD in WWI, were put up against a wall and shot for cowardice. So what did Struth do? He threw English back into the team almost immediately, not only worsening his condition, but making the player appear to be a heartless bastard, who was then taunted by other supporters as a 'murderer'. Looking at the bare facts known about Struth leads to only one conclusion; he was not a very nice individual.

Nowadays Struth would be called a control freak or even anal-retentive. His insistence on being in charge of every little detail, even down to the hats worn by his players, speaks of a petty-minded dictator. Even when he is painted in a good light it's hard to escape the conclusion that he wasn't a particularly likable man. But let's look at those words that always seem to be associated with him.

Dignity is a word that gets bandied about a lot at Ibrox; Walter Smith is often portrayed as dignity personified. This is despite the numerous times he lost his self-control and shouted at officials and other managers, even trying to physically attack Mixu Paatelainen. In fact, he once had to appear in court to face a charge of breach of the peace due to his behaviour. This is what passes for 'dignity' down Govan way. But what about Struth?

This is where 'honesty' comes into play. Struth, in his younger

112

days, was a professional athlete. One of the stories he liked to tell was about the time he cheated to win a race. This hardly paints him as a particularly honest individual. It does, however, point to what 'dignity' was and is all about at Ibrox: pretence. Swaggering about, looking sartorially elegant, looking down on everyone else and bragging how you're 'the best' while cheating to win at any cost seems to be what's required to qualify as 'dignified'.

'Openness' is hardly a word you would use to describe Struth, a man that played all his cards so close to his chest they left an imprint. This description was added by the Sons of Struth in a desperate attempt to claim the ghost of Struth in their anti-board stance. Again, Struth would be spinning in his grave. A man that was a petty tyrant and believed in unquestioning loyalty and forelock-tugging fealty would hardly applaud people that were fighting against their 'betters', would he?

Despite all the high-sounding epithets the Sons of Struth used about their hero, the essential truth was that he was the ultimate 'Real Rangers Man'; all bowler hats and bigotry. This was the type that they wanted at the top of the marble staircase.

As the months went on, the Sons of Struth became the boot boys for The Requisitioners. There were tales from people on blogs and newspaper forums of supporters being threatened by members of the Sons of Struth if they didn't join in the anti-board chanting. Instead of hatred of Catholics emanating from the Ibrox stands, all that was heard now were chants about spivs and crooks.

Of course, Leggat was all for the Sons of Struth and praised them to the Heavens. There's no need to point to specific instances; a perusal of his blogs during the latter half of 2013 will yield all manner of fawning over this group. Equally there is no need to point to individual blogs on McMurdo's site. A look at his blogs from the same period shows how he and his followers felt about the Sons of Struth. The divide was there for all to see.

Leading the Sons of Struth was one Craig Houston, who owned a cleaning firm but looked from his photographs like a Transylvanian funeral director.[3] He organised the Facebook page and the flashing of red cards at Ibrox and claimed that he had the majority of the support on his side.

Also involved was Sandy Chugg (now there's a name to conjure

113

with), a convicted drug dealer, who had once been the leader of a gang of hooligans called the ICF. He wrote a book about his thuggery, called 'Rangers and the Famous ICF'. Even the title says it all; they weren't just hooligans but 'simply the best' hooligans! Leggat wasn't about to let us know about this character's participation, especially since he frequently called pundit Stuart Cosgrove a 'former football hooligan'. It wouldn't do to look hypocritical, would it?

Both these individuals hardly fitted in with anyone's image of Bill Struth. Houston often looked as if he had been sleeping rough for days on end; understandable, perhaps, as nobody would want to look at that puss in a mirror. Chugg always looked like exactly what he was: a ned. Struth would have been horrified to see these characters using his name. An appearance of respectability was one of the dearest things to Struth's heart; the same could hardly be said about his spiritual 'sons'.

The big split in the Neo-Gers support was becoming increasingly bitter. McMurdo was being vilified on different forums, while his supporters had the same vitriol to spout about the Sons of Struth. Still, that would stop them having a go at everybody else, wouldn't it? Don't you believe it! Even though they now hated each other they still found time to agree that their troubles were all down to a grand conspiracy and that the other side in their internecine feud was playing into the hands of the 'Rangers-haters'.

McMurdo pointed to the Daily Record's championing of The Requisitioners' cause as evidence of this. The People generally viewed the Daily Record as being 'anti-Rangers' and pro-Celtic. Of course, they provided no evidence for this, mainly because none existed. McMurdo's contention was that since the Record was 'anti-Rangers' then it stood to reason that their stance against the board on the side of The Requisitioners was in order to destroy 'Rangers'.[4]

Leggat, predictably, took the opposing view. He said,

> Does any sane, rationale and thinking Rangers supporter really believe Celtic chief executive Peter Lawwell actually wants Paul Murray and the Nominees, with the return of Dave King and his millions to follow, plus the possibility of a Jim McColl investment in 2015?[5]

Rationale? When Leggat was a journalist his editor must have had a hell of a time making corrections!

They couldn't even fight with each other without bringing Celtic into it! So who would win the fight for the dark soul of Neo-Gers? Would it be the bigots? Or would it be the bigots? Whatever the outcome it was fun to watch!

21
Four Horsemen

It was a desperate last gamble. It was like the Magnificent Seven, except there were only four of them; four men, riding in to chase the spivs and crooks out of Dodge City. The peons cheered as the gangsters were going to be put to the sword and order would be restored. So who were these potential saviours?

First, we had Paul Murray. He had been on David Murray's Rangers board, giving him major kudos as one of the old guard. He had also been one of the Blue Knights, who had tried to buy Rangers during administration but were bumped in favour of Charles Green. Murray had distrusted Green, and all who came after, from Day 1, so his anti-board credentials were impeccable.

Next up was Malcolm Murray. Although he was tainted due to having been appointed by Green, this was mitigated by his subsequent boardroom battles with Charlie Boy and his friendship with Walter Smith. This Murray supposedly had an impressive CV, with many years' experience at the top end of the business world. This begs the question of what the hell he was doing still hanging about in Glasgow instead of being head-hunted by some top corporation!

Then we had the two folk nobody had ever heard of, apart from, I presume, their mammies. Scott Murdoch is apparently a successful businessman and was at that time a director of the Loch Lomond Golf Club. The other Mr Nobody was Alex Wilson, a former HR director with British Telecom. Both high-flyers in the business world, then!

To our agnivores in the press, the other three were an irrelevance; it was Paul Murray that mattered. Keith Jackson told us how Ibrox was 'a place where fear and confusion lurks in the dark shadows round every corner.' Well, what did he expect with a zombie club? Although I think Jackson was alluding more to the 'spectre of Craig Whyte and his bulging eyeballs'. There was only going to be one cure and that was The Requisitioners. As Jackson put it, Ibrox was a 'place where chaos continues to reign and will most likely do so until next month's long-awaited agm.'[1]

Of course, Jackson didn't bother to mention that it was the actions of Paul Murray and his cronies that had caused the AGM to be 'long-awaited'. He also didn't bother to mention, while he was mounting a personal attack on Whyte, that Jackson himself was instrumental in deluding The People into believing that Whyte was a man they could trust. It was Jackson that had coined the phrase, 'wealth off the radar,' after all.

And speaking of wealth off the radar, another in a long line of billionaires that were interested in the Ibrox club was behind The Requisitioners. Step forward Jim McColl. McColl had boasted at the end of October how he had the finances to 'take Rangers forward'. He spoke of many institutional investors that were desperate to put their money into Neo-Gers but did not want to line the pockets of Charles Green. This was why he was so keen to get his own men on the board.[2]

It seemed that anyone that was a millionaire, a billionaire or a business high-flyer wanted a piece of the Ibrox club. There was only one thing that they weren't prepared to do and that was put their hands in their pockets. Using your own money to invest was not the 'Rangers way'!

It had already emerged that David Murray had bought Rangers with other people's money and it's highly probable that Craig Whyte even borrowed the £1 that he handed over to Murray. Charlie Boy used borrowed money to buy the assets, which was paid back from the funds raised by the IPO. It seemed like Ibrox had been a magnet for a long line of tight-fisted, money-grabbing bastards. No wonder they kept waving those pish-stained sheets about in the Broomloan Stand!

If McColl was the billionaire that we were led to believe, then why didn't he just make an offer to buy shares? The price of the shares was nearly half of the IPO level, but there were those, like Sooperally, and Green himself, who had bought them for a penny and would still make a handsome profit. And some of the institutional investors might want to just cut their losses before the share price tumbled any further. It looked, though, as if McColl, like the rest of them, had short arms and deep pockets.

He might argue that he didn't want to line Green's pockets but that's how things work in the business world. Fergus McCann probably paid up for the Kellys' shares with gritted teeth but he still paid up. If McColl truly loved the club as he said, then surely that would come first above all other considerations? It appeared, though, that he'd rather see the club die than see the 'spivs and crooks' make any more money. He wasn't the first to try to take over the Blue Room without disturbing his bank account and he certainly wouldn't be the last!

This, however, mattered not a jot to The People and to the folk in our media. Bloggers like Leggat accused the board of all manner of dirty tricks, from PR guy Jack Irvine running a black propaganda campaign in the press to death threats against Jim McColl and his associates. When McColl pulled out of the whole thing, leaving The Requisitioners with nothing but his good wishes and a promise to turn up with funds if they were successful, Leggat was incandescent with rage. He recounted tales of telephone threats made to McColl and implied that this was the reason he had left the campaign.[3]

McMurdo ploughed his lonely furrow of backing the board, while Leggat accused him of being a mouthpiece for Jack Irvine, Leggat's new bête noir. He also said that McMurdo claimed to be the reincarnation of King Arthur's wizard, Merlin! Things were turning nasty.

To be fair to McMurdo, he had never claimed any such thing, although his weird theories about history left him wide open to scorn and ridicule. His madcap stories about Britain's destiny, the descent of British folk from the tribes of Israel and some arcane, magical future involving the Royal Family belonged more between the pages of a Harry Potter novel than a serious History book. Still, at least he made no magical claims for the Ibrox board!

It was hard for us outsiders to make out who had the most followers; the board or The Requisitioners. The multifarious supporters groups and their various blogs made it look like The Requistioners had the numerical advantage. It was unclear how many were in each of these groups, however, or how much overlap there was in membership. For all we knew there were only half-a-dozen of them making up all these different groups!

There was a large turn-out, though, for the Greetin' Meetin' held at the Grosvenor Hotel in Glasgow on 28th November. The meeting was chaired by Gordon Smith and was attended by all The Requisitioners. In between telling jokes about child abuse, they all agreed that Stockbridge must go, the Easdales must go; in fact, everybody must go! The crowd then went home to sharpen their pitchforks and get their blazing torches ready for the AGM on the 19th December.

Two weeks before the AGM, Keith Jackson was back on the case, telling the shareholders to vote for Paul Murray. He said that they should look, not at Murray's friends, but at the enemies he had made: 'Whyte, Duff and Phelps, David Grier, Green, Imran Ahmad, Craig Mather and Brian Stockbridge. None of them has a good word to say about Murray…This is the definitive Who's Who of the bogeymen in this unrelenting Rangers narrative.'[4]

From the start Murray had been trying to 'disseminate (I think Jackson means a different word there, maybe 'counter') the filthy lies of the Craig Whyte takeover'. Perhaps if a certain individual hadn't been convincing everyone of Whyte's massive wealth his job might have been easier! When Murray's Blue Knights were rebuffed in favour of Green (during administration, apparently; no mention of liquidation), Green was hailed as 'some sort of gruff- talking, big-handed messiah.'[5] Those with long memories will recall that Jackson was in the forefront of this as well.

Jackson made a last rallying call to the troops, and a major call to The Requisitioners to slam in the lamb if they won at the AGM. He painted a bleak tale of how far 'Rangers' had fallen, driven into a league where a game could be called off because of a crashed burger van. And who were the drivers? (Not of the burger van – the ones that drove 'Rangers' into the depths!) The club was apparently steered into this mire by a 'seemingly endless cast of pantomime villains'.[6] And who was going to rescue the club from this morass? Why, The Requisitioners, of course!

On Leggat's blog and other Neo-Gers sites, confidence was at a premium. The media might say that things were too close to call but the constant sniping at the board showed where their allegiances lay. The crowds of shareholders were going to march on Ibrox and take back their club. There would be rejoicing, dancing in the streets and lamb dinners for all!

We don't want to fight but by Jingo if we do,
We've got the ships, we've got the men, we've got the money
too.

And so the peons steeled themselves for the fight. Their pitchforks might be no match for the Gatling guns of the spivs but they had the Four Horsemen on their side: Yul Brynner, Steve McQueen, Charles Bronson and James Coburn. Nacho Novo had turned up at the Grosvenor to galvanise the villagers for the conflict. 'Keel the peeeeeeegs!' he yelled. Unfortunately, there was always the chance that they would just end up slipping and falling in a pile of shit from four horses!

22
Safe European Home

Charlie Boy looked to have gone for good, comfortably ensconced at Chateau Vert in France. Just down the road, in Monaco, Craig Whyte was well out of things as well. According to many, however, they were both still involved at Ibrox. Certainly Green still had his shares, which Laxey and the Easdales couldn't take off his hands until the end of December. With all the suspicions about Green being linked with Whyte it was easy to argue that Craigie was involved as well.

Whether it was out-of-body experience or astral projection, it seemed that the spirit of Whyte was haunting the corridors of Ibrox.[1] The place should have been safe with the stern-faced ghost of Bill Struth to look after it but he was no match for Whyte. Perhaps the ghost of William Wilton, oar-blade still stuck in the back of his head, was helping make Struth's afterlife a misery!

The result of the 'independent' inquiry into Whyte's involvement at Ibrox had shown that there was nothing to worry about. There were a few facts pertaining to the inquiry, however, that made The People distinctly uneasy. The first was that Deloitte was involved. Deloitte helped Green, Ahmad and Stockbridge when they took over at Ibrox and were also involved in the share issue. Not only that, but they also happened to be Green's personal tax advisers.[2] They hardly appeared independent, did they?

Throughout the inquiry both Green and Whyte refused point-blank to co-operate. Whyte particularly was advised by his legal team not to get involved. The inquiry's investigators searched computer files, laptops and mobile phone records in order to find out whether or not Whyte was still involved.[3] But if Whyte and Green refused to co-operate then whose records were the investigators looking at? It all seemed like an expensive waste of time and allayed nobody's fears.

The third problem with the inquiry was that nobody got to see the report. The directors at Ibrox would have seen a copy but we don't even know if the SFA were given the full report or if they just took the Ibrox directors' word for it. If there was nothing to hide, then surely the whole document would have been handed over to the press so as to stick two fingers up to all the critics of the board? The fact that they didn't, and that the whole thing was shrouded in secrecy, meant that speculation continued unabated.

The major concern of The People, and the reason for all the accusations of the board being full of spivs and crooks, was the amount of money that the club had gone through. When the accounts were finally published it confirmed the suspicions of many that Neo-Gers was just one big gravy train. The current board would have to be ousted and quickly.

Everyone went on about all the snouts in the trough but appeared to ignore the biggest snout of all. Sooperally used his huge, porcine arse to shove everybody else out of the way and make sure he got more swill down his gullet than the rest. His massive salary and pocketful of penny shares went unremarked by all but the 'Rangers haters'. Once his salary was out in the open, Sooper promised to take a wage cut but, as time went on, there was no sign of it happening. Sooperally escaped censure while those in the boardroom were reviled by all and sundry. Even The Requisitioners themselves had nothing to say about Sooperally and his Soopersalary.

So what, exactly, were The Requisitioners going to do differently from the current board? Surely the whole situation called for cutbacks and the club living within its means? But that wasn't what Paul Murray and his gang were proposing at all. Malcolm Murray claimed that he had institutional investors lining up to put their money in, although he wouldn't tell us who they were.[4] Maybe Adidas and the Dallas Cowboys were going to be involved!

Paul Murray also spoke about strengthening the team, although he had a plan for this based on all the money that would be flooding in.[5] Despite his claims about a gradualist approach he would have realised that The People wouldn't stand for that. 'Back' to the top and stopping Celtic was all the Neo-Gers support cared about so, if Murray and his Requisitioners wanted to keep The People onside they would have to spend, spend, spend.

So there it was: mystery investors and a war chest for Sooperally. Essentially, if The Requisitioners took over it was just going to be more of the same. So what the hell was the point? Well, as everyone in the press was saying, the ones involved in the new club so far had all been completely untrustworthy.

It was easy to point the finger at Green and his French chateau, but what about Whyte? It's difficult to see how much Whyte is supposed to have creamed off during his tenure. If anything it could be argued that Whyte did his best to save Rangers and if it hadn't been for him then administration and liquidation would have come a lot sooner. If Sooperally hadn't been so useless then Rangers might have been in Europe and everything would have worked out fine; but, then, nobody was going to blame the Cheeky Chappie for anything, were they?

As for the unpaid PAYE, Whyte was just carrying on the Ibrox tradition of not doing taxes. If Whyte hadn't withheld this cash, then Jelavic would have gone a lot sooner and half the team would have had to be sold in the January window. Even when he sold the Arsenal shares it looked as if Whyte ploughed the money back into the club. But administration and liquidation happened on Whyte's shift so, to The People and the agnivores he was to blame for everything.

It's hard to see what Whyte got out of his ownership of Rangers and, looking back at the string of failed companies he trails behind him, the guy hardly looks like anyone's idea of a successful businessman. His castle in Scotland was even repossessed because he couldn't keep up mortgage repayments. To all intents and purposes Whyte is just a loser in a suit. I wonder what it is he does in Monte Carlo. I bet he
stands around on street corners, selling Le Big Issue!

Back to The Requisitioners and it was easy to see why they were receiving so much support from the Sons of Struth and the agnivores in the press, despite the fact they had nothing new to offer. They were 'Real Rangers Men' and, really, that was the only difference between them and the current board. Being a 'Real Rangers Man' was also the reason why Sooperally had no finger of blame pointing in his direction.

23
The Equaliser

While this War of the (Blue) Noses was going on, a wee, obsessive man sat in a small, lonely bedroom in a flat in Belfast. He was sickened, not by what had happened to his old club or what was happening to his new one, but with what everybody had been saying about Rangers. The accusations of being cheats, tax dodgers and the rest were, to him, totally unjustified and inaccurate. Like the rest of The People, he believed that the Lord Nimmo-Smith report had proven Rangers' innocence. All the stuff about them being cheats was obviously motivated by bigotry, hatred and envy. He was going to show them. He was going to show everybody!

He started downloading everything he could find about Celtic's finances and sat, long into the night, poring over every document he could lay his hands on. Night after night he sat, studying accounts, land deals, loans, anything he could get, until his eyes and head ached. Fortunately, he had no job and no friends, so he could afford to spend all this time on his obsession. His mother let him be. She was overjoyed in thinking he was finally showing an interest in women and was happy to let him sit wanking over internet porn in peace.

As his tired eyes and befuddled brain searched through document after document, he thought he discerned something amiss. How much had Celtic paid for those bits of land they had acquired? What terms had been agreed for the loans Celtic had got from the Co-operative Bank? The more he looked the more convinced he became that he was on to something. He needed more evidence.

He bombarded Glasgow City Council with requests for documents under Freedom of Information legislation. As each pile of papers arrived he hurriedly scanned through them for more items to fit with his theories. His mother watched him disappear into his bedroom with the plain paper packages, a twinkle in her eye and a smile on her lips. He was in his forties and going thin on top but, at last, he was going through puberty!

As his narrative took shape he began to post his ideas on Neo-Gers websites. He discovered that there were others just as obsessed as he was; especially somebody that ran a website called Football Tax Havens. This gave him confidence to continue with his research and his revelations on the internet caused excitement among many of The People.

It was all very well, however, preaching to the converted. He needed to get word out to the wider world to show that Celtic was as bad as, if not worse, than Rangers had ever been. He considered his options. He could start his own blog but, again, he would just be telling one group of people what they wanted to hear. What about the newspapers or other media? They were all in the grip of Celtic-loving, Republican-supporting, liberal-minded Fenians. He'd get no help from them. Then it struck him. He would go to Stormont and seek the aid of his MP, or, indeed, any MP that would listen to him.

Fortunately, everything was quiet in Northern Ireland these days. The Troubles were over and everyone was now living in peace and harmony. The MPs, most of whom shared their time between Westminster and Stormont, had nothing to do but sit around all day scratching their arses. One MP jumped at the chance of something to do and promised to follow follow the case, yea, even unto the halls of Westminster.

Proudly the wee man was able to announce, on McMurdo's blog, that a written question had been handed in to the Chancellor of the Exchequer concerning Celtic's dealings with the Co-operative Bank. It was all going to come out now and Celtic would be finished.

A quick search through Hansard online revealed that the questioner was one Gregory Campbell, Democratic Unionist Party MP for East Londonderry. He asked the Chancellor if he would 'investigate reports that the Co-Operative Bank provided exceptionally low-interest-rate loans and overdraft facilities to Celtic Football Club.'[1]

Practically everybody in the House of Commons was probably sick of hearing about Celtic from Gregory Campbell. He was constantly bringing up questions about them and asking the House to condemn them. Still, it was better than what concerned him in Northern Ireland, where he and his colleagues were against abortion and vehemently anti-gay. One of his friends in the DUP claimed that the recent terrible floods in England were a punishment from God for allowing same-sex marriages!

Campbell is also a firm believer in Creationism, which he wants promoted in the schools and museums in Northern Ireland. Since Creationists believe that the world has only been in existence for six thousand years, they totally reject that dinosaurs died out millions of years ago. They are often pilloried for books showing people living with dinosaurs. Campbell will have the last laugh, though. He runs a stable of dinosaurs in County Derry and is hoping to enter a tyrannosaurus in next year's Cheltenham Gold Cup. He recently ran this tyrannosaurus at Fairyhouse but the race was abandoned when the brute started to eat the other jockeys.

To Campbell's dismay, and that of the wee man in Belfast, the question was answered in the House of Commons on the 6th January 2014. Sajid Javid, the Financial Secretary to the Treasury, reiterated that the Government was ordering an investigation into the Co-operative Bank. That was the good news. The bad news was that, 'Individual commercial loans are a matter for agreement between the parties concerned.'[2]

So that was that line closed. But the wee Belfast man still had his land deals between Glasgow City Council and Celtic to cling onto. He still received encouragement from The People on the internet so he persevered.

As the investigations of the wee Belfast man and Football Tax Havens continued, questions began to be asked by The People about why our mainstream media wasn't reporting all this. It was a rhetorical question as they already knew the answer: Peter Lawwell had the press in his pocket. The facts, however, were rather more prosaic.

I've already said why none of the papers reported on the Charlotte Fakes revelations; they were terrified to in light of the Leveson Inquiry. The same now applied to these accusations and allegations. Nobody wanted to end up in the dock like Rebekah Brooks.

After The People inundated the European Commission with demands for an investigation into Celtic's 'state aid,' the papers did report when the EC carried out preliminary enquiries, as it was duty-bound to do. These enquiries were to judge if there was anything worth investigating. The People, however, used their usual hyperbole and declared that Celtic was under investigation.

Although the newspapers didn't report any of this stuff, it didn't stop The People from posting on online newspaper forums as if Celtic had already been found guilty. With childlike glee they prophesied the end of Celtic Football Club. But surely they didn't want Celtic to be gone when their club got 'back where it belonged'? After all, they wouldn't want to win all those 'tainted titles,' would they?

The truth was that they wanted to drag Celtic, if not the whole of Scottish football into the gutter with their new team. It was to be like *Götterdämmerung* in Wagner's *Der Ring des Nibelungen* opera. This is the last part of the opera and outlines the death of the gods and the destruction of Valhalla. Everything perishes with them. Adolf Hitler was affected deeply by this opera and it's thought that his prolonging of the war when it was obvious that Germany had lost was influenced by the *Götterdämmerung;* he wanted to bring everything crashing down with him. Now The People wanted to do the same with Scottish football.

Unfortunately for them, there was another major reason why the newspapers wouldn't touch these allegations; they were a load of Craig Whyte! Figures were conjured up that bore no relation to what had actually been paid, Glasgow City Council was named as the sellers when the vendors were actually the Greater Glasgow Health Board and Dunbartonshire Council. Folk with Irish-sounding names, who had signed various documents, were called Celtic season-ticket holders. It was all getting a bit desperate.

Even more desperate was when they suddenly became champions of architectural heritage and lovers of wildlife, even though the royal family that they all revere is systematically attempting to wipe out most of the species on these islands. This was all about London Road Primary School; the wee school that stood in front of Celtic Park.

It seemed that Celtic had bought this old school and might even demolish it. The People started to shed tears over the destruction of this beautiful and culturally important old building.

I suppose when you attend a place like Ibrox, which is falling apart round your ears then any building looks beautiful and culturally important. The truth was, however, that London Road Primary was neither beautiful nor culturally important. It was an old dump, long past its best-before date.

I worked at this school for a short time and the classrooms were tiny and cramped, built for a bygone age when children sat in rows and didn't dare either move or speak. It was a nightmare trying to organise desks for modern-day group teaching. The children were great but had more than their fair share of fights and scrapes in the playground, mainly because it was so small, again a legacy of Victorian times. The atrium had the large stairwell over it and had such an echo that it was difficult to even have a conversation. The only one that liked it was one deaf lad, who liked to stay inside at playtime and make loud noises, which he could hear reverberating all round the building.

Celtic offered their facilities for the school to use, for football training, sports days and the like. The head teacher of the school was off sick long-term so a senior teacher was in charge. She had a horror story to tell.

The summer before I started there, which would have made it June 1995, the senior teacher decided to take Celtic up on their kind offer and hold the school sports day in Celtic Park. Many parents were unhappy about this and some of them kept their children off that day but, still, a reasonable-sized crowd went along. The ground staff, aided by one or two players, couldn't have been more helpful. They provided things like marker cones and disks and anything else that was needed and helped out with organising the games. Many of the parents scowled but things went okay.

The trouble started when the games were finished. Some of the Celtic staff came out with free juice, crisps and bars of chocolate for all the kids. Of course, the crisps and chocolate bore the Celtic emblem, which enraged many of the parents. About half the children had the treats cruelly snatched away from them and dumped in a bin, while the senior teacher looked on in embarrassment. Needless to say, she didn't bother taking the children back to Celtic Park after that episode!

With such bigotry so openly on display, it was hardly surprising that I met with some strange scenarios in the classroom. I remember teaching one of my Primary 2 boys about multiplication. The rest of

128

his group had picked it up and were getting on with their work, but this lad was a bit slow on the uptake. I put two sets of different amounts of cubes in front of him, explaining to him that this is what 'two times' meant. Understanding eventually dawned in his eyes so I put two sets of three in front of him and asked him what 'two threes' were. After a few seconds hesitation, he announced his answer.

'Five,' he said.

'Eh?' I asked him to show me why.

He proceeded to count each cube individually while pointing to it, '1, 2, 3, 4, 5!'

'What about that one?' I asked, pointing to the cube he had missed out.

'Oh, Ah'm no' countin' that wan!' he replied matter-of-factly. 'It's green!'

Anyway, I'm away off the subject. Suffice it to say that London Road Primary was not a great building for teaching and it certainly wasn't beautiful, or culturally important for that matter. It wasn't designed by Rennie Mackintosh, like
Scotland Street School and I've worked in a lot more beautiful old buildings, Elmvale Primary in Springburn for one.

The desperation of The People to save this 'wonderful building' even extended to bombarding wildlife organisations with e-mails, demanding to know if the building had been checked to see if there were bats living in it!

Nothing has come of the EC enquiries as yet and when they do declare that there's nothing to investigate we'll no doubt hear how Peter Lawwell has the European Union in his pocket! In the meantime, they're all still punting these allegations as if they're fact. We mustn't laugh, though. As Frankie Howerd was fond of saying, 'It is wicked to mock the afflicted.'

24
Clampdown

I wonder if anybody remembers Jo Moore. She had worked as a press secretary to the Labour Party and ended up as special advisor to Stephen Byers, the Transport, Local Government and Regions Secretary. In 2001 when the World Trade Centre was attacked, Moore sent an e-mail to her department's press office, saying, 'It's now a very good day to get out anything we want to bury. Councillors' expenses?' This e-mail was sent while the tragedy was still unfolding, before either of the Twin Towers had collapsed.[1] When the contents of this e-mail were discovered it was universally condemned as the worst example of 'spin' ever.

Now it appeared that the same cynical maneuvers were being used in the fight for control of the Blue Room. Leggat (who else?) told how Jack Irvine, the Ibrox PR man, had used a major story to bury bad news about the Neo-gers board. In fact, he went further by claiming that the major story had actually been set up by Irvine from the start.

At the Celtic AGM on November 15th 2013 there were a couple of serious issues up for debate, issues that had been forced onto the agenda by ordinary Celtic shareholders. One was that the club should pay staff the 'living' wage instead of just the minimum. The other was about how Neo-Gers had been dealt with by the SFA; the resolution called for Celtic to bring in UEFA to look into this matter.

These were issues that the board wanted to sidestep. Accordingly, the AGM was conducted in a light-hearted way, with plenty of jokes. One joke, however, didn't go down too well at Ibrox, or with the agnivores in the press. Peter Lawwell, when asked about Neo-Gers being the 'same club,' joked, 'Rory Bremner can pretend to be Tony Blair.' The press was outraged, as were The People and the Ibrox boardroom. Believe it or not, Neo-Gers actually reported Lawwell to Vincent Lunny, the SFA's compliance officer!

This is a normal reaction for The People and the powers-that-be at Ibrox. It's always hilarious when they call Celtic supporters 'the easily offended' or the 'perma-offended'; it doesn't take much to get The People riled and if there's nothing there to rile them then they'll make it up. For example, Alex Thomson called them 'daleks' because they always seem to be of one mind and shout the same slogans. To The People, however, this was a reference to the Ibrox Disaster since everyone knows that daleks can't climb stairs!

Anyway, Leggat took a different view from that of his fellow People. He saw Lawwell's joke as a diversionary tactic to help cover up bad news concerning the Neo-Gers board. Jack Irvine's name crops up again and, although Leggat doesn't say explicitly that Irvine and Lawwell were working together, the implication is there. Apparently Lawwell was afraid of The Requisitioners taking over at Ibrox and building a strong Neo-Gers, so his joke was a ploy so that Irvine could bury the news of Scott Gardiner turning down the job of CEO at Ibrox à la Jo Moore.[2]

According to Leggat, Irvine was busy clamping down on all negative stories concerning the board. Journalists were having their arms twisted so that they would be more pro-board and anti-Requisitioners. It just shows the paranoia of Leggat and The People in general that they couldn't just look at a newspaper. If they had they would have discovered that if Leggat, and other bloggers, were right about Irvine then whatever he was doing wasn't working. The press was manifestly on the side of The Requisitioners.

To McMurdo it was the spin doctors on the other side that were getting our media to do their bidding. Not that they needed to; our media were already perfectly in tune with the need for 'Real Rangers Men' at Ibrox. Whether it was PR people at work or not, some of the press activity was a bit suspect to say the least.

In October 2013 the Daily Record ran a piece about the huge house that Stockbridge had bought in Dunbartonshire, a well-heeled area to the north-west of Glasgow. Presumably the guy wasn't a pauper before he came to Ibrox so there wasn't anything unusual about him buying a house in Bearsden or Milngavie or wherever it was. Most people with a good salary and a family want to live there since you get the best of both worlds; you get to pay a minuscule amount of council tax while still being able to take advantage of all the free things that Glasgow has to offer.

The implication in the Daily Record article, however, was that

Stockbridge had been able to buy his 'mansion' due to all the money he had accrued on the Ibrox gravy train.[3] Just in case any of the wilder elements of those that supported The Requisitioners wanted to do something about it, the Daily Record helpfully published a picture of Stockbridge's house.[4]

Leggat kept banging on about how Jack Irvine was going all-out to make sure that the board got a good press and their enemies were painted as the villains of the piece. If Leggat was right then it has to be said that Irvine's reputation as a successful, hard-hitting PR man was undeserved. Whatever PR job was being done on behalf of the Neo-Gers board was obviously an abject failure.

Oh, and the result of the complaint to the SFA about Lawwell's joke? It was thrown out as being a waste of time.[5] This was the view of Campbell Ogilvie, the SFA president; and him a 'Real Ranger Man' too! What was the world coming to?

25
Know Your Rights

At last the big day arrived. There was excitement in the air as all the blue-nosed *sans-culottes* got ready to storm the battlements and remove the hated regime. I was going to keep going with my metaphor and say *Ancien Regime*, but that's what they were trying to restore!

My metaphorical French Revolution is not too wide of the mark, particularly where the bloggers were concerned. McMurdo had already, away back in October, called the ones following The Requistioners socialists. He meant this as a slur, calling socialism the politics of 'spite and envy toward those with a few bob'. He also cast some disgusting aspersions towards the Red Clydesiders in the process.[1]

Leggat, of course, saw things much the same but with a different slant. To him it was the forces of democracy against a malign dictatorship. He said, 'Any Rangers supporter who is also a shareholder must now act. Every Rangers supporter who is also a shareholder must make sure they vote on Thursday.'[2] According to Leggat the vote was going to be tight and everybody was needed to fight the good fight.

When The Requisitioners went to court to get the AGM postponed, a spokesman for them said, 'It is ridiculous that we are forced into going to the Court of Session in order to give the shareholders a democratic vote at the AGM.'[3] So, even according to The Requisitioners, it was all about democracy.

There was speculation about which way Sooperally would vote. The members of the board were his employers and he had done extremely well out of them: a huge salary and a big bag of penny shares. On the other hand, The Requisitioners were his pals, especially Paul Murray, who was from the good old days. What was he going to do? True to form, he took the sleekit way out. He handed his proxy over to a fans' group so he could avoid all responsibility. The fans' group might vote against the board, but

Sooper could claim, 'It wisnae me!' Then again, they might vote *for* the board but Sooper could still turn around and say to his pals, 'It wisnae me!'

As usual, however, nobody would say a bad word against the Cheeky Chappie. The CEO, Graham Wallace, said that he 'understood' why Sooperally had done it and that the manager still had the 'unanimous support of the board'.[4] The other side was, understandably, overjoyed; the supporters' groups and The Requisitioners praising Sooperally to the hilt.[5]

Leggat went completely overboard. He spoke of Sooper's 'Struth credentials,' how he had 'stood tall' and had 'rallied a stunned support'. Leggat also pointed out how Richard Gough had come out to condemn the current board.[6] We would be hearing a lot more from Gough as time went on.

On the day itself, the Daily Record printed a last-minute rallying of the troops by Paul Murray. Even though there had been a leak a couple of days before saying that the board was going to win, Murray discounted this as scaremongering tactics to put people off turning up. He said, 'This club does not belong to the current board. It never has. It belongs to the fans.' He used the Big Lie to appeal to his supporters. 'It was not Charles Green who saved the club after Craig Whyte tipped it under. It was the fans who saved it by buying season tickets and rallying to the cause.'[7]

He obviously forgot, like everybody else, that nobody saved the club; it went into liquidation. What he was trying to take over was actually a new club; Green's club. And if Green hadn't set in motion the Big Lie then it's doubtful that anybody would have bought season tickets. But I suppose we'll never know. Unless, of course, the new club goes tits-up as well.

And so The People turned up at Ibrox, pitchforks and ploughshares at the ready. They cheered their four heroes and booed the villain, Brian Stockbridge. Since this war had started James Easdale and Stocbridge had begun to get lonely in the boardroom so they brought some others in. There was Graham Wallace, the CEO, whom everybody seemed to trust; The Requisitioners had made noises about keeping him on and Jim McColl had expressed faith in him. Next we had David Somers, the Chairman, a man whose face seemed to be all chins. Then there was Norman Crighton, a non-executive director in charge of bringing in investment.

The meeting was a rowdy affair, with Brian Stockbridge unable to speak without being booed. Angry questions were thrown at the board as everyone geared up for the vote on the resolutions to elect the Four Horsemen onto that august body. The Murrays and their two cronies must have felt smug as they watched the anger reach fever pitch around them. They were going to be a shoo-in for places on the board. Unfortunately, they, and their supporters, had made a serious miscalculation.

Democracy, one man, or one person, one vote is the only fair way to run a state. If you don't like what your government is doing, then you can kick them out come the next general election. All true freedom-loving people will do anything to protect their democracy, even if they don't always like the government that has been elected.

Unfortunately, democracy can't work in every situation. Can you imagine if a vote had to be taken in the armed forces every time a decision was to be made? If that had been the case back in the 1930s and 1940s we'd all be speaking German now. Then again, there needn't be a vote on every issue; we could elect the commanding officers of our armed forces. Surely that would work?

In Ancient Athens, from where we get our democratic ideas, generals were voted in and could easily be voted out. This could cause major problems when a minor setback could cause a general to be kicked out right in the middle of a war. Look up a guy called Alcibiades and you'll find out how fickle the Athenian democracy could be. (You'll also enjoy reading about one of History's greatest characters!)

In our society a general would have to make a complete and utter arse of things before being removed. Commanding officers need to be given a chance. Imagine if all our armed forces' commanders had been booted out after Dunkirk, which, no matter what spin is put on it, was a defeat. Would we still have won the war?

As well as inheriting our political systems from Ancient Athens we've also inherited many of our legal systems from Ancient Rome, no matter what the likes of McMurdo might tell you! One of the main tenets of Roman law was a complete respect for private property and business. In fact, much of the Roman tax system was put out to private tender. To the Romans state business and private business were totally separate and, of course, different systems existed to run them.

The Roman Republic may have become a bit more democratic over time but private business was a different matter. Shareholders decided who would run a company; not on a one-man-one-vote basis but on the basis that it was shares that counted. If you owned a majority of the shares, then you decided who ran the company and how it should be run.

There's a point to all this showing off I'm doing about my knowledge of ancient history. That point is that The Requisitioners were remarkably naïve. For such supposedly high-flying businessmen they showed an amazing lack of nous. I know next to bugger all about business but even I knew right from the start that they were heading for a bruising.

The fact is that James Easdale didn't own enough shares to keep himself on the board so he must have been receiving the support of the institutional investors. If they had thought that he was doing a poor job then they'd have already kicked him, and Stockbridge, out on the street. The fact that they hadn't proved that he had their full support. So, when it came to the vote, all Easdale had to do was slap his proxies on the table and that was it, the game was a-bogey.

The institutional investors were the ones that The Requisitioners should have been sucking up to. They tried, but they didn't try hard enough. A major stumbling block, however, was the fact that nobody had any idea who some of the institutional investors were. Who was behind Margarita and Blue Pitch Holdings? The fact that The Requisitioners couldn't even find out who the investors were should have set alarm bells ringing; they didn't stand a chance!

The problem now was that they had riled up The People for nothing. They had stirred up a great deal of anger and hatred and gained absolutely zero in the process. As Pandora discovered, once you've opened the box that's it; the demons you've released will never go back in.

The Sons of Struth, the Union Bears, the Rangers Supporters Trust and all the rest of them had been told by The Requisitioners and everybody in the media that they were the ones that had saved 'Rangers' and it was their club. They had been promised power only to see it snatched away. Now there was no way they were going back in their box. Their anger still remained and they went back to waving their red cards, old towels and pishy bedsheets. All it needed was somebody with a bit more savvy than The Requisitioners to come along and The People could be used again.

Leggat disappeared in the mother of all huffs, like Rumpelstiltskin when the queen says his name, or maybe 'Merlin' McMurdo cast a spell on him. More likely than not, however, both he and Jabba were off, propping up a bar somewhere in North Lanarkshire, regaling a pub-full of bored listeners with stories of the good old days in the 'inky trade'.

26
One More Time

January 2014 started quietly, but this was Neo-Gers we're talking about so it couldn't last. Sure enough, the big story soon broke about Neo-Gers players being asked to take a fifteen-percent pay cut. Of course, the players told Graham Wallace where to stick his pay cut. Well, they maybe didn't go that far but they refused to take the pay cut nonetheless.[1] Neo-Gers tried to play down the request, Wallace saying that the request put to the players was just him considering 'options in order to move this club towards sustainability.'[2] Despite what Wallace said, the speculation soon started to mount that administration was coming to Ibrox again.

Suddenly the floodgates were open and the stories came thick and fast. Craig Whyte reappeared, claiming that he still owned all the assets. He had been banned for life from having anything to do with any football club in Scotland but he said that this ban would not hold up in court. His case was going to see 'significant movement…in the next few weeks'.[3]

Sandy Easdale responded in belligerent fashion, saying that all the shareholders had more of a claim on the assets than Whyte did. This was a simplistic view of things; if the courts were to support Whyte's contention that Green's acquisition had been illegal then there wouldn't be any shareholders! Still, Easdale promised, in true Charlie Endell style, that if Whyte showed up at Ibrox he 'personally would throw him down the marble stair case'.[4] Obviously the board was still desperately trying to appeal to the lowest common denominator among The People.

At the AGM in December Graham Wallace announced that he was going to do a 120-day review of the whole business from top to bottom. This would theoretically give the board some breathing space since any criticisms could be countered with 'wait until the review is finished.' Theoretically was the operative word. The demonstrations against the board continued apace and the smell of pish from all those sheets in the Broomloan Stand became the norm at Ibrox.

Meanwhile, the Ibrox board had decided that the best way to cut back on the expenditure at Neo-Gers was to employ somebody else. Phillip Nash was recruited as a consultant to start streamlining the club.[5] Only at Ibrox would they think it was a good idea to fork out extra money in the name of cost-cutting. Nash had worked previously for Liverpool and Arsenal so he probably wouldn't come cheap. With this board in place the Broomloan Stand bedsheet wavers didn't have far to look for ammunition.

Then there was Damille, who bought two million shares in Neo-Gers from Richard Hughes of Zeus Capital. Like Laxey, Damille was a hedge fund group.[6] They were supposed to be 'turnaround specialists,' which seemed a good sign, until you stopped to consider what having 'turnaround specialists' in a company usually entailed. There's an excellent documentary series, by producer/writer/director Adam Curtis, called 'The Mayfair Set', which sets out exactly what so-called 'turnaround specialists' do. They sell off unprofitable parts of a company, cut the workforce and shed assets. The bit that's left shows a profit, share prices increase and they can make a killing selling their shares before everybody realises that they've bought shares in a much-reduced company. The series is available on YouTube and I thoroughly recommend it.[7]

Such people are hardly the types you'd want involved in any company and certainly not a football club. Besides, hedge funds only exist to make money for their investors and are rarely in any kind of venture for the long haul. A great crowd to welcome to Ibrox; they'd have been better off with Charles Green!

As if these stories weren't bad enough, details emerged of the Neo-Gers team's preparations for a Monday-night game against Forfar. They had lunch at the four-star Carnoustie Hotel and stayed on so that the players could take advantage of all the facilities the hotel had to offer, including rooms where the poor, overworked souls could go and rest before the 'big game'. Sooperally provided us with some comedy when he came out with his excuses. 'The Forfar players were away for a pre-match meal as well.'[8] I wonder, however, what the Forfar players had for their pre-match meal; probably a Pot Noodle and a can of Irn Bru in the changing room!

Astonishingly there were no apologies forthcoming from Sooper;

as far as he was concerned he had done nothing wrong. He said, 'We are still Rangers Football Club and have always attempted to be as professional as we can.'[9] And therein lay the problem. As a supporter pointed out, 'We are the biggest club in Scotland so why should we not act professional before games?'[10] The fact is, however, that there's nothing at all 'professional' in living beyond one's means. The reality was that it was all for show; act as if you're a big club and folk will believe you're a big club. It was certainly at odds with the board's professed desire to streamline the whole operation. For Sooper, the team and many of the supporters all that seemed to matter was appearances. There's the influence of Struth again! But there was more to it than that.

This ridiculous expenditure was all part-and-parcel of the pretence that this new club was still Rangers; and Rangers had to behave according to its status. The argument that they were the 'biggest club in Scotland' was nonsense, but they all believed it nonetheless. More to convince themselves, rather than others, that it was still Rangers, then it had to act like Rangers. If that meant overspending on trivial luxuries, then so be it. For the Big Lie to work, the club had to appear to be able to carry on the way it used to. It was like a family that all dresses in designer clothes to show off, while secretly living on nothing but bread and frozen chips from Iceland. There were a few noises of dissent but The Review would sort everything out, wouldn't it?

More of a concern to Sooperally was the fact that the transfer window was open and the worry that top teams in England would come 'swooping' for his team of world beaters. Only one player attracted any scouts; Nottingham Forest expressed an interest in Lee Wallace, eventually tabling a bid that came to nearly £1 million with add-ons. Surprisingly, Neo-Gers turned down the offer, demanding £1.4m. Forest decided to go elsewhere, a spokesman saying, 'Forest won't pay another penny for a player from Scottish football's third tier.'[11]

So that was that; there would be no cash coming into Ibrox during the transfer window. Nobody was interested in the rest of the team, even, to everyone's utter amazement, 'prolific goalscorer' Lee McCulloch. But, wait a minute, what's that? A last-minute bid for Nicky Law? According to Sooperally, Graham Wallace threw out the bid for being derisory. It seemed that somebody was trying to take advantage of the financial situation at Ibrox.[12] Rumour had it that Blackpool, under caretaker manager Barry Ferguson, came in with a bid of £50,000.[13] What a bloody cheek, eh?

It seemed to have been forgotten by The People and their friends in the press that Neo-Gers had tried the exact same tactic with Hearts back in 2012. Charlie Boy tried to take advantage of the situation at Hearts by offering them £500,000 of the £800,000 still owed for Lee Wallace. Our old friend Jabba said at the time that Hearts should have been biting Green's hand off and wondered what they were playing at.[14] Strangely, nobody was saying that now about Neo-Gers; but, of course, The Review was going to sort everything.

Graham Wallace decided to throw a bone to the bedsheet-wavers and get rid of Brian Stockbridge. Of course, he 'resigned' from his position but the statement to the Stock Exchange said that he had left 'by mutual consent'[15] so it wasn't as if he had suddenly decided to fall on his sword. His departure meant that all three of Leggat's 'Three Musketeers' had now gone, victims in the quest for 'Real Rangers Men'.

Speaking of the bedsheet-wavers, an old friend of theirs turned up again in January, hovering over the dying carcass of Neo-Gers. Dave King was back! But what was he up to? The Ibrox boardroom was desperately in need of cash and King, reportedly, had cash to spare and then some; so why weren't the two of them getting together? Keith Jackson put it down to those in charge at Ibrox wanting to cling onto power and not wanting to dilute their shares by selling any to King.[16] Whatever the reason, King looked to be just hanging about doing nothing; but looks can be deceptive!

One point that Jackson made sure to emphasise was that none of the financial mess was Sooperally's doing. As Jackson put it, 'the real culprits behind this club's overspending have been based in the boardroom, not the dressing room.'[17] He had a point; Brian Stockbridge, for example, had been on a huge salary as well as sizable bonuses.[18] Then again, the same thing could be said about Sooperally.

An integral part of the Big Lie was that Sooper had been the manager of Rangers and was still the manager of Rangers. That being the case, or, rather, the story being given out, then Sooper couldn't possibly have his salary reduced. If that happened, then they would have to admit that the new club was, in fact, a new club. To maintain the illusion that the club was still Rangers, Sooper was still being paid the same wages he'd been getting in 2011. Not only that, he was raking in bonuses and preferential share deals as well.

Comparing Sooper with Stockbridge, however, was hardly comparing like with like. Not unless Brian Stockbridge was enjoying meals, saunas and afternoon naps in swanky hotels at the club's expense. That mattered not to Keith Jackson. Fingers couldn't be pointed at Sooper; he was a 'Real Rangers Man', wasn't he? Just like Dave King, in fact.

27
Movers and Shakers

Graham Wallace had assured everybody at the triumphant AGM that there was no chance of the club going into administration, even though Brian Stockbridge had said that there would only be a million quid left in the bank come April.[1] Even in January Wallace was still bullish. 'Come April we'd be confident that the club will have sufficient cash in the bank in order to maintain our operations,' he said.[2] So it appeared that everything was hunky-dory and there was nothing to worry about. And then, in February, came a bombshell.

It was announced to the Stock Exchange that Neo-Gers had borrowed money to see the club through for the next couple of months, until the season-ticket money started to come through. £500,000 was borrowed from Sandy Easdale. This loan was interest-free but was secured against Edmiston House and the Albion car park. Also secured against these assets was a loan of £1 million from Laxey Partners. This one wasn't interest-free but would earn Laxey £150,000. Both loans were due to be repaid by September 1st.[3]

The only reason why a lender would ask such a high interest-rate or demand that the loans were secured was because there was a high risk of the loans not being repaid. This would look bad enough if it were a bank or even a pay-day loan company handing over the cash, but these lenders were actual shareholders! It certainly didn't augur well for the club's future.

Imran Ahmad, meanwhile, appeared back on the scene. He had been claiming since he left that the club owed him money, a bonus for securing investment. He went to court to get the £500,000 he said he was owed 'ring-fenced' in case Neo-Gers went tits-up just like the old club. The judge, Lord Tyre, refused, quoting the loans recently secured by Neo-Gers as his excuse.[4] This was rather strange reasoning by the judge; surely he should have taken into account the circumstances and the stringent conditions of the loans when deciding the financial fitness of Neo-Gers?

Anyway, the Neo-Gers board soon had more to worry about than

Ahmad and his half-million quid; Dave King had finally decided to show his hand. He called for supporters to withhold their season-ticket money until the board gave assurances about the future of Neo-Gers.[5] He also claimed to have offered investment to the board but that his offer was rejected. What, exactly, his offer entailed he omitted to say.

According to David Somers, the chairman of Neo-Gers, all King had done was express an interest in any future share issue. He had come up with no scheme for investing his cash other than that.[6] So who were The People supposed to believe?

All the rhetoric about the board being full of spivs and crooks had gone on so long that practically everyone took it for granted now. Charles Green's French chateau stood as a monument to the gravy-train culture that had gone on, and was continuing to go on, at Ibrox. On the other hand, were they to trust a man that a South African judge had described as a 'glib and shameless liar'?[7]

The new anti-board mob, calling itself the Union of Fans, were quick to support King's call for withholding season-ticket money, even asking him to set up some kind of mechanism to operate it. 'We cannot doubt the intentions of one of our own who has previously committed £20m to the club we love,' said their statement.[8] Craig Houston of the Sons of Struth, which had now been subsumed into the Union of Fans, said of King that 'The fans see him as the knight coming over the hill to help.'[9] It looked like the board had another fight on its hands.

Quite why The People should place their trust in King was a mystery to those of us on the outside; it seemed to all hinge on that phrase 'one of our own'. He was a 'Real Rangers Man' and that was enough. There was also the little matter of the £20m he had invested in Rangers and lost. In 2008, when the South African Revenue Service was chasing King for all the tax he owed, a South African business newspaper, the Weekender, quoted the assets and income that SARS had assessed. One of these was 200m Rand that was income from Rangers Football Club.[10] I looked up the exchange rate for the end of 2008 and this comes in as the best part of fifteen million quid! It looks as if King might not have lost as much as he makes out.

And what plans did King have for Neo-Gers? He spoke of injecting money, and more money so as to fix the team and the crumbling stadium. He played up to the fears of The People, 'If we cut our costs to suit our present income, we will remain a small club and Celtic will shoot through 10 in a row - and beyond - while we slug it out for the minor places.'[11] That sounded pretty much the same as what The Requisitioners had been saying.

Not for King, however, the rough-and-tumble of a shareholders' meeting and a battle that, like The Requisitioners, he was bound to lose. He had a more direct approach to ousting the board: he was going to starve them out.

Keith Jackson came straight out and said why so many might support King.

> King, they say to a man, remains…to use another home-grown term, the embodiment of a "Rangers man". It is this one basic credential above all others that separates King from the succession of fly by nights, chancers and opportunists who have at one stage or another taken on lead roles in this seemingly endless Ibrox narrative.[12]

No prizes for guessing whose side Jackson was on then!

Sooperally dodged the question of which side he was on when asked straight out. It was also put to him if he understood why the fans might look to him for guidance.

'Absolutely, he said. (Now there's a surprise!) 'And you can understand that while I'm sitting here, all I will be talking about is football.'[13] Maybe he should have proxied his decision to a supporters' group!

Jackson, meanwhile, continued with his hero worship, 'If these supporters cannot place their hopes and trust in one of their own, then all trust and all hope might perish for good.'[14] Now there was a rallying call for The People to get behind a 'Real Rangers Man' if ever there was one!

The bedsheet-wavers shouted all the more against the board now that they had somebody to lead them, a 'Real Rangers Man' with wealth off the radar! They also decided to increase the temperature of the online war of words against McMurdo etc. Things were getting so out of hand that even the police were getting involved.[15] With the reputation of The People for violence it probably wouldn't be long before somebody got hurt.

28
The Right Profile

As early as January legal threats from Ibrox caused the Sons of Struth website to be closed down.[1] Lawyers' letters continued to fly about and Craig Houston, leader of the Sons of Struth, claimed that he was going to be dragged to the Court of Session and taken for everything he had.[2] Other 'rebel' leaders, like Mark Dingwall and Chris 'Ze List' Graham told similar stories of legal threats against them. Dingwall said, 'It seems that anyone who opposes the board is subjected to legal threats or complaints to the police. It is heavy handed. This is a campaign of harassment designed to shut down legitimate debate.'[3]

The real story was, however, that the Easdales had had enough. It wasn't the attacks against the board that were the problem; it was the personal, potentially libellous, attacks that constantly appeared on these blogs and Facebook pages that the Easdales took exception to. It's easy to say that you didn't write the offensive statements and to point to a disclaimer on your site but, ultimately, you are responsible for what appears on your website. If you're going to allow all manner of abuse on your site, then hell mend ye! To be honest, these clowns were lucky that all they woke up to was the postman bringing a lawyer's letter, instead of a horse's head on the pillow next to them. (Only joking, Sandy! Only joking!)

It turned out that Houston was right to be worried about being taken to the Court of Session. Sandy Easdale explained that 'This is action I am taking personally for libellous comments about me,' and that he had 'sent several nice lawyers' letters asking to stop and we'll forget about it.'[4] Unfortunately, Houston hadn't complied so now it was no more Mr Nice Guy.

To provide some kind of sop to the 'rebels' the Ibrox board got rid of Jack Irvine 'by mutual consent'.[5] It was too little too late, however, since The People and the agnivores already had

146

their 'Rangers Man' in Dave King. All the lawyers' letters in the world couldn't change the fact that that King was being held up as the acme of integrity next to all the 'spivs' at Ibrox.

In reality, if even half the stories doing the rounds about King were true, then he was much more of a gangster than the Easdales could ever be. His name was being linked to characters that it's hard to believe exist outside a Hollywood movie. International, organised crime syndicates, illegal cartels, folk on the FBI's 'most wamted' list; King's name kept cropping up. And it wasn't just gangsters from Africa he was supposed to be connected with, but from the Middle East and Far East as well.

The judiciary in South Africa hadn't just been concerned with tax when King started to be investigated; they were also looking at charges 'ranging from racketeering to fraud'.[6] Many of these charges had to be dropped because of missing witnesses or procedural problems with evidence; the kind of thing you'd associate with the Mafia. But even on the strength of what King actually was convicted of he makes Sandy Easdale look like a choir boy. (I was going to say 'altar boy' but…) And yet our media frequently painted Easdale as 'convicted fraudster Sandy Easdale,' while lying through their teeth that King had 'settled' his dispute with SARS. Not that there was any kind of agenda or anything, you understand!

Dave King came out with a statement in March, tearing lumps out the board and giving clear hints that he was going to start up this 'Trust' for the Neo-Gers supporters to put their season-book money into. He had been told by the board that the terms of the Laxey loan, including the collateral, were necessary because of a 'combination of legal risk and the current financial position'. (That's weird; Lord Tyre told Imran Ahmad that everything was okay!) King said that the same conditions applied to season-ticket money and that said money, once paid in, should be 'ring-fenced'.[7]

I don't think I'd ever heard that term, 'ring-fenced', until this whole sorry saga started. I think it was when Whyte was still around that we started hearing about 'ring-fenced funds'. Since then it has cropped up in just about every chapter of the Rangers and Neo-Gers story. Anyway, I digress.

The Union of Fans agreed with everything King said, of course, and vowed to go ahead with setting up the Trust Fund. In the meantime, they promised to back off with their campaigns until The Review was finished. They were still going to plan for the Trust Fund, however, in case it was needed.[8]

There were a lot of questions that needed to be answered about this planned Trust Fund. The idea was that the fund would drip-feed the money to the board on a match-by-match basis. Since buying match tickets singly was a good deal more expensive than buying a season book, where was the extra money going to come from? Not only that, but how could anybody putting their season-ticket money into a fund be guaranteed that they'd be able to get the seat that their arse had occupied for years? And that's even before the biggest question of all; was it safe to hand over your hard-earned to a convicted crook?

McMurdo claimed that fans were contacting the club to confirm that they would be renewing their season tickets. Not only that, but some of them were promising to buy extra books to make sure that the board got the funds it needed. According to McMurdo the number of supporters putting their money into the Trust Fund was going to be 'pitifully small'.[9] That remained to be seen.

Meanwhile, Craig Houston had received a summons from Sandy Easdale's solicitor, telling him that he was going to be taken to court for £200,000 damages.[10] Although that's less than two months' wages for Sooperally, it's not an amount that we mere mortals usually have lying about the house. Understandably, Houston was a bit upset but he lost quite a few friends by demanding to know why Easdale wasn't suing the owners of some other websites. Opinion appeared to be divided about Houston but one thing came through loud and clear: Easdale wasn't a 'Real Rangers Man'.[11]

Weirdly they were all up in arms about Easdale taking legal action, considering his reaction over-the-top for a bit of name-calling. There was a touch of the pots and kettles about this; after all, what was the reaction of The People anytime anyone mentioned the phrase 'new club'? There was also the fact that

148

there was rather more to this than a bit of 'name-calling'.

I'd never heard of the Easdales until they arrived at Ibrox and started appearing in the papers. There were a few rumours about them being 'gangsters' and, as I said before, they certainly looked the part. On my blog, therefore, I usually referred to them as 'The Krays'. This was in a joking context, however, and I used comedic names for all the participants in the Ibrox drama. I doubt if this kind of thing would bother Sandy Easdale. Nor would his brother, James, be bothered about the various Celtic websites that poked fun at his hair. Was it or wasn't it? Whether it was a syrup or not, his Alvin Stardust style kept everyone amused!

The websites of Houston and others, however, were a different matter entirely. On these sites the brothers were accused of being pimps, money launderers, drug dealers and worse.[12] There was no joke intended in these posts so it was hardly surprising when the Easdales decided that enough was enough.

The People that supported the board, and a lot of others besides, were outraged when it emerged that money from the Rangers Fans Fighting Fund was going to be used to help pay for Houston's defence.[13] As it turned out, Sandy Easdale dropped his case so the money wasn't needed but this could have caused a serious split in the anti-board faction. Obviously Sandy didn't do his research properly or he would have known about this massive difference of opinion. If he'd continued with his threat, then he could have driven a wedge into the anti-board faction and left them squabbling and fighting among themselves.

Keith Jackson decided to use a bit of psychology in his latest attempt to drum up support for King. He brought out the Ghost of Christmas Future to terrify The People. Who was going to stop Celtic from marching triumphantly to ten-in-a-row?[14] He warmed to his main theme a couple of days later when he questioned the trust that the Neo-Gers had for Graham Wallace. 'The longer King is kept at arm's length the less trust these fans will have for Wallace and his regime,' he said.[15] A quick search on the internet would easily have shown

149

who was the more trustworthy. And contacting a few pension fund operators and the like in South Africa would have garnered the advice that arm's length wasn't nearly far enough to keep Dave King.

In the minds of the agnivores, however, and, indeed, of many of The Peeppul, money wasn't everything. King was originally from Castlemilk, claimed to have supported Rangers since childhood, had invested in the club when David Murray owned it and been on the board. His credentials as a 'Real Rangers Man' were, seemingly, impeccable. That was why they wanted him to take over; all the other so-called reasons for supporting him were nothing but rationalisations. And who cared if he was a crook and a gangster? In fact, surely 'talents' such as he had might come in useful in running Neo-Gers.

29
Time is Tight

'This is not just your seat. You are keeping it warm for the generations to come. Because Rangers Football Club is bigger than any individual.' So went the sales pitch on the Neo-Gers website. It was time to renew those season tickets.

It was the second week in April and there were still a few weeks to go until The Review became public. The conundrum for The People was whether or not to renew until they had seen what The Review had to say. The renewal forms had to be in by May 6th so would that give folk the time to mull things over once they'd read The Review?[1] And what about those that paid in instalments? If they didn't get their forms in to cancel by 28th April, then the first direct debit would come out of their accounts automatically.[2] It looked like their decision was being taken out of their hands.

Many of The People were already well pissed-off. Sooper had managed to get his team to the final of the Ramsden's Cup this year but were beaten by Raith Rovers. Sooper's team had played their usual tactic of fannying about until the other team got tired. Unfortunately for them, the Rovers team has professionals in their midst and are used to playing against teams in the Championship. The People went home completely stunned; this match had been considered a foregone conclusion.

To add insult to injury, Sooper and his team went to a party after the game. While The People were lying in bed with their heads stuck under the quilt asking why, Sooper and his team were belting out 'Why, why, why?' at a karaoke. Once the singing was over, and everybody was well-oiled, the party continued with a disco.[3] To say the Neo-Gers fans were angry is an understatement. The Daily Record phone-line was red hot.

'McCoist is a disgrace as a Rangers manager. What previous manager would be partying after a humiliation?'

'The Rangers manager has taken more out of his club in the last two years than anybody else. For what? Two part-time leagues?'

'I was out on Sunday for 16 hours to travel to the Ramsdens Cup Final and finally got home at 12.30am after watching a spineless and gutless display by Rangers. I was seething. Then to rub it in our faces McCoist goes on the drink with the players. Time's up Ally, go now.'[4]

Sooperally was unrepentant about the party, saying that's what they always did after a cup final, win or lose. He stated, 'We were all unhappy, very unhappy. Every one of us, fans, players, staff, every one of us. That's all I would say on it, nothing more.'[5] Well, he certainly didn't look too miserable in the leaked photo of him belting out a tune at the karaoke!

Less than a week later came the Scottish Cup semi-final against Dundee United. The People were not very optimistic but as the day approached they started to get a bit of their arrogance back. They were going to have home advantage, playing at Ibrox, weren't they? Perhaps the game against Raith was just a hiccup. There were even rumours that the pitch at Ibrox was being narrowed to stop United playing their usual wide game. The People started to talk about going to Celtic Park for the final. Reality hit home with a vengeance when Dundee United beat them 3-1.

All this combined to make buying a new season book a less attractive proposition than it had appeared the year before. Yes, Neo-Gers would be marching into the Championship but the inexorable, smooth journey 'back' to the Premiership was looking less and less like a foregone conclusion. There was also another consideration; one that The People would never admit to. A clue to their worries was contained in the advert for season-ticket sales; that bit about keeping a seat warm for future generations.

The same rhetoric had been used in the early 1990s when David Murray had sold, not just season books, but actual, real, physical seats at Ibrox. Nameplates were put on the seats and the idea was that the seat could be passed on down the generations.

Debentures, these contracts were called, and they raised a great deal of money. To The People, though, it wasn't just a cynical money-raiser; they felt like they owned a little bit of Ibrox. The idea was an appealing one; future generations sitting in the same seat that their grandfathers' and great-grandfathers' arses had occupied. It spoke to The People's obsessions with traditions. And then came administration.

Suddenly, those debentures weren't worth anything at all and, as 2012 progressed, it became evident that generations of arses weren't going to be enjoying those seats. Apparently, the debenture contracts weren't with the club at all, but with some mystical company that had been running Rangers for 113 years without anybody noticing. Of course, the debenture holders could have argued their case that their contracts had been with the club; that, however, would have struck at the very heart of the Big Lie.

It must have stuck in many of The People's throats when they saw that new advert for season books. Keeping a seat warm for future generations had turned out a complete sham previously; who was to say it wouldn't turn out to be a waste of money this time around too? It was certainly something else to hold against the Neo-Gers board.

As if that wasn't bad enough there were the interim accounts that were published at the end of March. These showed a loss of £3.5m from July to December 2013. The auditor, Deloitte, of 'Independent Inquiry into Whyte' fame, warned that if fans withheld season-book money then there was a possibility that Neo-Gers might cease trading.[6] In other words, the Frankenstein monster made out of the body parts of Rangers might itself die.

This wasn't going to deter the Union of Fans, though; if anything it made them all the more determined since there was every chance of getting rid of the board. They were going ahead with their plans for a Trust Fund, which they claimed was supported by thousands of fans. We've already looked at the risks involved in this venture as far as the fans were concerned but there was another consideration that those thinking about joining in had to take on board: the sheer madness of the scheme.

There was nothing particularly mad about the Trust Fund per se, but it was the demands made by the Union of Fans that

153

should have given pause to any potential contributors. What they were demanding was security over Ibrox Stadium and Murray Park![7] It's a bit like somebody trying to demand security over their local shop before handing any cash over for purchases. You can just imagine the scenario.

'Alright, Mr Patel? I'm just here to pay for my papers. Here, was that you I saw coming out of the bank yesterday?'

'Yes. I needed a loan to tide me over for a bit. They made me put up my van as collateral.'

'Is that right? Maybe you'd better sign the deeds of your shop over to me before I pay for these papers. I need a guarantee that the money will be ring-fenced for the paperboy instead of you taking it.'

Their demands really were as ridiculous as that. They were customers and their season-book money was payment for a product: a seat to watch their team. It wasn't a bank loan to be repaid or a mortgage or anything of the sort; it was a customer paying a business for a service. In essence the whole 'Trust Fund' palaver was nothing short of blackmail.

And then more news came out to annoy the already incensed People; they wouldn't be able to pay by credit or debit card when buying their season tickets. The company that processed card transactions considered the club to be at risk and demanded security over Ibrox Stadium before they would deal with any payments. Graham Wallace blamed this squarely on the plans to withhold season-ticket money, which he said had frightened the company off.[8] So it was cash only, unless you paid in instalments; it looked like the company that dealt with credit payments were carrying on as normal.

The calls to wait until The Review was made public began to sound more desperate and forlorn. It was like some exasperated mother telling her children to wait till their father got home. It was beginning to be feared that perhaps The Review wasn't going to be the panacea that everyone had thought.

154

The Neo-Gers board was thinking along the same lines and seemed to be expecting to have a fight on its hands. To help they recruited a new PR man, Paul Tyrrell, who had a reputation as a bit of a bruiser when it came to spin.[9] As I said on my blog at the time, Tyrrell was more 'truculent bam' than 'succulent lamb'. If they needed a guy like this on their side, then obviously The Review was not going to make pleasant reading.

30
The Call Up

At last the great day arrived and The Review was published. All you could really say about it was, 'Holy shit, Batman!' It showed that Neo-Gers had burned its way through £70 million in the less than two years since its inception. Some sources insisted that it was 'only' £67m but the £70m figure became the accepted sum, probably because the number '67' is a bit of a sore point with The People! Excuses were made about one-off purchases but it was still a hell of a lot of money. Astonishingly, included in the money spent was Green's initial payment to Duff and Phelps for the assets. Then again, maybe that wasn't so surprising; it seemed that nobody ever bought into Ibrox with their own cash.

Of course, all this prodigality was blamed on Green and everyone else that had comprised the old board. Some folk tried to pin some of the blame onto the Easdales, but James Easdale had only joined the board the previous summer, while the same was true for Sandy Easdale on the football board. Most of the £70m had been spent well before they got their feet under the table.

McMurdo professed to see some positive things about The Review: it was an honest assessment and it showed the way forward.[1] This, however, was clutching at straws. Yes, cuts would have to be made but a child could have worked that out in 120 seconds, never mind 120 days! And what about investment? Yes, Wallace was saying that investment was needed and would be brought in, but, as usual, there was no mention of who these investors might be or what strategy was going to be used to entice them.

Probably the best thing that could be said about Wallace's plans was that King's weren't much better. He had finally come out in March to say that he was willing to invest £30m of his own money over four years. He said that the club needed £50m but that he 'could probably get other people to put in £20m.'[2] Well, that sounded a bit 'Dallas Cowboys,' didn't it? He also banged on about another share issue[3] so perhaps he wasn't going to risk his own cash after all!

156

Whatever King said or didn't say, there was no denying that The Review was a godsend to the Union of Fans. Even they hadn't reckoned on the losses being as bad as £70m! And just to put the tin hat on things it transpired that Wallace's accusations about the threatened season-ticket boycott causing the lack of credit and debit card facilities was a load of Craig Whyte. In fact, the company that conducted the card transactions had demanded Ibrox Stadium as security away back in January. Wallace had to squirm and go back on his previous statements, claiming that it was just 'negative comment in the media' that he had been talking about.[4]

The Union of Fans, meanwhile, had their website set up for supporters to start the process of putting their season-ticket money into the promised Trust Fund. They called the site, and the fund, Ibrox 1972, presumably after their old club's European Cup-Winners' Cup win. A statement on the Neo-Gers website called it 'a worthless academic exercise created to serve the purposes of individuals and not the greater good of Rangers Football Club'.[5]

Richard Gough had climbed on the Dave King express to lash out at the board and to act as a trustee of the Trust Fund. Not everyone was happy with this as they remembered Gough saying that Rangers had died. Surely he couldn't be a 'Real Rangers Man' if he'd come out with something like that? (They always seem to forget that Walter Smith said more or less the same thing.)

Gough phoned McMurdo to put his side of the story across. He explained that when he said that 'the club I gave blood, sweat and tears for is dead,' what he was really talking about was that the 'era' was dead. He went out of his way to stress that the club playing at Ibrox was still Rangers.[6]

Here are a few snippets of what Richard Gough actually said in 2012.

I'm still numb by the news 140 years of history has been wiped out in one fell swoop. It's like a death in the family you know has been coming for a while.

I hope they show no mercy to the people who have destroyed Rangers.

It's not just the graveyard of Rangers these people are dancing on…'[7]

I'd say all that was pretty unequivocal. Gough said that Rangers were dead and no amount of weasely backtracking can change that fact.

Surprisingly, Imran Ahmad was blocked yet again in his quest to get the money he was claiming ring-fenced. Lord Armstrong ruled that although there was 'some scope for concern' there was no proof that Neo-Gers might be insolvent by 2015 when Ahmad's case was due to be heard.[8] This was an even worse decision that the earlier one by Lord Tyre. Fans were withholding season-ticket money, which Deloitte had warned might lead to insolvency, a company was demanding security over the stadium before it would do business with the club and there were already two loans secured on assets. I would consider this rather more than 'some scope for concern'!

The Truculent Bam, Paul Tyrrell didn't seem to be doing too much to earn his corn. Graham Wallace was wheeled out for a Q & A session on Twitter and proceeded to make a complete fanny of himself. Even Jabba couldn't have done it any better!

The Q & A session was billed under the hashtag 'ReadyToListen'. (Remember that silly survey? Another chance for jokers to send all manner of ridiculous suggestions.) Wallace might have been ready to listen but, as it turned out, he didn't have very much to say. He hummed and hawed his way through, desperately trying to give nothing away and resorting to platitudes about everything being fine.[9] If this exercise was supposed to get everyone onto the board's side, then it failed miserably. Wallace's evasive answers would see to that. For example, when asked why bonuses were being paid when redundancies were occurring, Wallace could only say:

> We are restructuring areas to better position us for future growth. As part of this, a small number of roles may be affected. We are working with everyone potentially impacted to identify if there are any potential alternatives for them.[10]

As you get in Parliament, there were a few questions that were obvious plants, only asked to make the board look good, like the one asking if Wallace would be coming to NARSA that year, and another asking if the Ibrox lavvies were going to be spruced up a bit. There was even a question about how difficult Wallace's job was with all the negative stories in the media. Gary Ralston, in the Daily Record, was quick to highlight some of the questions that *hadn't* been answered, or even acknowledged:

> What exactly are Sandy Easdale's roles and duties? Who is he answerable to? Who ok d him to do interviews?
>
> Can you confirm Charles Green no longer has any ties to the club?
>
> Why can't bonuses to yourself or any other directors be scrapped completely or withheld until we are stable?[11]

In the meantime, there were ex-Rangers employees queuing up to give vocal support to Dave King. Alex McLeish claimed that the fans were right to demand security over Ibrox, saying that 'it just seems like common sense'.[12] That was a strange thing to say! Next up was Lorenzo Amoruso. He waxed lyrical about 'spitting blood' and said that the board 'had to go'. And then came the clincher; he said, 'I want the Rangers family back.'[13] So there we had it; bring back the 'Real Rangers Men' and everything would be fine!

Last but not least was Nacho Novo. We hadn't heard from him since his star turn at the child-abuse joke-fest in December. He added to the call for 'Real Rangers Men,' saying, 'I have been supporting King and before him Paul Murray, they are Rangers people and for me I will always side with them.'[14] There was no mistaking what his take on the situation was, then!

Oh, almost forgot, there was one more ex-player that came out in support of King. Bomber Brown squeezed himself into his dad's old suit again to speak to the press. Speaking of Murray Park, he said, 'The fans should demand it is given over to their safekeeping.'[15] And the board was just going to acquiesce to that, wasn't it? Besides, wasn't he the one that claimed that there was a question mark over who actually held the deeds to Ibrox? How was the board supposed to hand it over if they didn't own it?

While this big love-in was taking place, McMurdo pointed out a fatal flaw in the argument for 'Real Rangers Men'. If, as the Union of Fans maintained, the Blue Room had been full of 'crooks' and 'spivs' that 'stole' the best part of £70m, then Walter Smith and his pal, Malcolm Murray had to be labelled with one of those terms as well. Either that or they were completely incompetent in chairing a boardroom full of criminals.[16] Obviously the Union of Fans hadn't considered this.

But, then again, maybe they did consider it. If there's one thing you can say about The People, it's that they're not overly endowed with brain cells. They had accepted it without question when Malcolm Murray, as part of The Requisitioners, claimed to have had no part in all the shenanigans that he accused the board of. No doubt they would accept without question the same reassurances from Walter Smith. And then there was the biggest question mark of all against their intelligence: handing over their money to a convicted criminal to avoid giving it to other folk that they thought might be crooks!

31
Police on my Back

No sooner had we got the chance to read The Review than Graham Wallace was facing a police investigation. A shareholder, who also happened to be a banker, had reported Wallace to the police, accusing him of breaching the Companies Act. His alleged crime was that he had misled shareholders at the AGM in December. He had told the meeting that the club had enough funds to last it until the end of May but then had had to borrow £1.5m in February. The accusation was that he had obviously lied to the shareholders.[1]

A Neo-Gers statement said, 'Mr Wallace has no knowledge of a complaint, which, if put to the club, has no grounds.'[2] To paraphrase Mandy Rice-Davies, they would say that, wouldn't they? On the other hand, when the loans were taken out it was termed as being an 'emergency' loan. Now the thing about an emergency is that it's something that you don't see coming; otherwise, it wouldn't be an emergency, would it? Maybe Wallace had thought there was enough money in December but something unforeseen happened in February. If all else failed, however, Wallace could always blame it all on Green.

Keith Jackson's reaction to all this was predictable. He advised Wallace to resign immediately. He said that Wallace 'ought to remove himself from this omnishambles'. (I wonder where he got that word, 'omnishambles'? I don't think it's a real word at all; it was made up by one Phil Mac Giolla Bhain.) Jackson also had a pop at the Easdales, saying that they had been in charge for twelve of the eighteen months of money being lost. And then there was the lack of financial security at a time when 'Dave King continues to sit in a corner on a bundle of cash'.[3] You would think that he'd have learned his lesson about selling millionaires and billionaires to The People!

And the rozzers were called in again when another shareholder, who had demanded to see the service contracts of the current directors, complained when he was refused access. The board changed its mind and allowed the shareholder in. He then wanted to see contract details for Charles Green and Imran Ahmad, but the board refused, saying that his request was 'time-barred'. Under Company Law they are only required to disclose contract details for the past twelve months. The shareholder maintained that both Green and Ahmad had remained as directors at least until the end of May 2013. So it was back to the police.[4]

One thing this shareholder did discover was that Graham Wallace was on £315,000 a year and was possibly in line for a 100% bonus on top of that.[5] That was a lot of cash but still nowhere near Sooperally's hefty wage packet, even with that bonus! Still, The People were incensed; what the hell was the bonus for?

Wallace himself pointed out that he may only get some, or none, of the outlined bonus. 'Any bonus that I may be awarded would be discretionary, based on a mix of company and personal performance.'[6] That would make it bugger all, then; unless, of course that 'personal performance' clause includes things we don't know about. The mind boggles.

Meanwhile Sandy Easdale's lawyer was busy sending out letters again and to the same recipient, Craig Houston. Houston had set up an e-petition for folk to sign if they backed the call for Ibrox not to be sold or used as security for loans. Fair enough, but every time somebody signed up, an e-mail was sent to Sandy Easdale. Apparently it was his personal e-mail address this stuff was being sent to.[7] It could be claimed that it was no big deal but that kind of thing can be bloody annoying.

On the other hand, it's an easy matter to block e-mails coming from a particular source, or even to change your settings so they're sent to the 'spam' folder. It doesn't take a genius to work this stuff out but, if you're a complete technophobe, you could always ask somebody else to do it for you. There must be somebody at Ibrox, surely, that knows how to work a computer? Maybe the person had already been let go as part of the cost-cutting. But, then again, the most important skill for working in the Ibrox offices has always been prowess with a paper shredder!

In all probability, though, it was the hand of Paul Tyrrell that was behind this move. I mentioned before that Easdale had missed a golden opportunity to drive a wedge among the anti-board sheet-wavers. The news that the ones in charge of the Fans' Fighting Fund had promised to use some of the money for Houston's defence on the last occasion had caused uproar. If I could see that this was a chance to get one over on the Sons of Struth then I'm sure it was obvious to somebody like Tyrrell. Houston had vowed that he wasn't going to stop the e-mails being sent to Easdale, so it was going to be interesting to see what happened next.

While all this skullduggery was going on it looked like the season-ticket renewals weren't going that well. Nobody was giving out any figures, least of all at Ibrox, so there probably weren't that many folk buying them or they'd have been trumpeting it to the skies. Some estimates put the figure as low as 2,000, but it was sheer guesswork; there was no way of finding out the true figures.

One indication of how badly things were going was that the secured loans apparently hadn't been paid back yet. After the furore over the Laxey deal, Neo-Gers transferred the loan to a fan, one George Letham, who handed over the £1m while only asking for half the amount of interest that Laxey had demanded. Luckily, Laxey were happy to go along with this new deal. The loan was set up under the same terms and was to be paid back as soon as season-ticket sales brought in enough to do so.

By the 25th May, however, over a week after the extended deadline for renewals had passed, Letham had still not received his money or any indication as to when he would be getting it.[8] The only conclusion that could be drawn from this was that not enough season books had been bought. Granted, many supporters might have chosen to pay in four instalments, a facility brought in when First Data refused to handle credit-card transactions. This would leave Neo-Gers effectively skint, with nobody like Ticketus around anymore to cough up some cash up front.

The loan from Letham, and the £500,000 one from Sandy Easdale, remember, were secured against Edmiston House and the Albion Car Park. What would happen if the board couldn't scrape the money together before September 1st? Still, there was the open sale of season books to come in June; there might still be hope.

Paradoxically, there was no crowing about numbers from the Union of Fans either. Their 'Ibrox 1972' website gave no indication of how the Trust Fund was doing. You'd think if they had thousands

163

signing up then they'd want to brag about it but there was nothing to see at all.[9] So what was going on; were The People supporting the boycott or not?

A clue to what was going on came in a couple of the comments on McMurdo's blog.[10] It seemed that there were a lot of The People that were not bothering to renew their season books because they agreed with Craig Whyte's assessment of Sooperally; i.e. 'he's fucking useless!' As long as Sooper was in charge they could see the next season's matches being just as boring as last season's, with the added worry that the team was going to be skelped senseless by the professional teams in the Championship.

Of course, these folk that were not renewing because of Sooperally were not going to hand over their cash to Honest Dave's lack-of-trust trust fund. They might have been daft, but they weren't stupid!

As for the various threatened court cases and calls to the police, it's interesting to note that nothing ever became of them. We rarely read of anyone abandoning their legal moves or, if we did, there was no explanation as to why. From big headlines in the papers, especially the Daily Record, most of these stories just seemed to disappear. You'd expect somebody to say that they were now satisfied and weren't pursuing the matter anymore, or that they were still incensed and were taking it to the very top; but no. Strange, eh? Or, then again, perhaps not.

Did anyone on either side of the war really want the police or the judiciary poking about at Ibrox? King, the Sons of Struth, McMurdo and his mob, the current Neo-Gers board, even Leggat might all hate each other with a passion but they all had one thing in common: The Big Lie. No matter whether you wanted 'Real Rangers Men' in the Blue Room or found the sight of brown brogues anathema, you had to agree on that one point. Nothing could be allowed to interfere with the fallacy that the club now occupying Ibrox was 'still Rangers'. This would explain why Sandy Easdale's solicitor's letters came to nothing; his corporate backers were probably having none of it.

The board, meanwhile, probably had no fears of that banker actually going ahead with his 'police investigation'. That individual would no more want official noses getting involved than the board or the big investors. So, why did the board acquiesce and let him in to look over at least some of the books? That's easily explained. The battle for control was mostly being played out in the media. The mystery investors behind Neo-Gers didn't want any publicity at all, whether bad or good. If that banker fellow had continued to be knocked back, then the Daily Record would have been all over it. Better to give in a little than have a light shone where nobody wanted it.

As for the Sons of Struth, they weren't in the least interested in the police or the courts. The pishy-bedsheet displays seemed to suit them just fine.

32
The Street Parade

On Saturday 24th May 2014 the Sons of Struth held a protest march to Ibrox stadium. They had their red cards at the ready for the photo shoot and then they were going to hand them in at the Ibrox ticket office. Apparently 400 people turned up, which Craig Houston said he was really pleased about, having expected 'that there would maybe only be 100-200 so the numbers that have turned up for the first event of many this summer are very encouraging.'[1] The BBC put the figure that turned up at around 500,[2] so it looked like quite a good crowd for 3pm on a Saturday. A look at the video of the march, however, tells a different story.[3]

That's quite a crowd outside the Louden at the start of the video. But wait a minute…a lot of those folk probably have got nothing to do with any marches; they're just outside the pub and the bookies for a fag! Then there's the march along Mafeking Street, where there seem to be a lot more folk at the start than there are at the finish. I think some of those people were either just going to their cars or taking a shortcut home. Some of them look like elderly gentlemen, who were probably rushing home to try to explain to the missus why that 'quick pint' took three hours!

Once they reach Ibrox they're probably lucky if there are 200 folk there. Craig Houston is doing his best to make the crowd look bigger, shouting through his megaphone, 'Fur fuck's sake, wull yez spread oot!' Of course, when they all gather together to hold their banner up, the paucity of numbers is evident.

Whoever organised the event obviously didn't put too much thought into it. When they went to do their stuff at the ticket office there was nobody there for them to snub and the doors were locked. They had to form their queue on the stairs, which kind of defeated the whole point of the exercise.

Then they discovered that there was nowhere for them to stick their red cards. Well, I'm sure Sandy Easdale could have come up with a few suggestions but I doubt they'd have been welcome. Instead, they all wandered round to the main door at Argyle House to shove them through the letterbox. And that was it. Oh, a wee man came out to ask them what the hell they were playing at; that was all the attention they got at Ibrox.

This anti-climax came at the end of a couple of weeks of drama when it looked like the Union of Fans might actually have won. The Ibrox board caved in and invited representatives of the rebel group for talks. On offer was, not the security over Ibrox being signed over, but a legally-binding agreement that the stadium would not be sold or used as security for loans. A triumphant Chris 'Ze List' Graham crowed, 'We made it clear to Mr Wallace we felt it was also appropriate they provide the same undertaking for Murray Park.'[4] Graham Wallace promised to discuss it with the other directors.

Unfortunately, this didn't go down too well with the faction that had supported the board all along. They felt 'taken for granted' and betrayed by this seeming capitulation. Even the fact that the board was actually talking to the Union of Fans was a slap in the face. There were dark mutterings of folk now planning not to renew their season tickets because of this craven behaviour.[5] It looked like the board couldn't do anything right!

One day later and everything was back the way it had been before. The board hadn't bothered to get back in touch with the Union of Fans so there was no deal. Craig Houston sounded worried. 'I just hope that the fans don't get spooked into renewing at the last minute.'[6] There wasn't much chance of that, though. It looked like just about all of The People were pissed off at the board for one reason or another, or at Sooperally for being 'fucking useless'.

And so, by the looks of things, neither the board nor the Union of Fans had won. The board didn't have the money to pay back its loans but the paltry crowd of folk at the march showed that there wasn't the mass support for the rebels as everyone seemed to think. The fact that there was no boasting on the Union of Fans website either would suggest that they had nothing, in fact, to boast about!

On 30th May Craig Houston and Bomber Brown turned up at Ibrox with a petition to demand assurances about the stadium.[7] I would imagine that nobody opened the door; I mean, have you seen that pair? Both of them are scary-looking fuckers so it's hardly going to fill anyone with joy to see them turn up at the front door together. Neo-Gers later released a statement to say that Halloween was not for another five months.

The actual petition itself had just over 7000 names on it. Not very impressive, is it? Considering that this was an online petition there should have been far more names than that. What happened to the 'global' fan-base? I think part of the problem was that they could only find 7000 of The People that were able to write their own names or knew how to turn on a computer.

The lack of enthusiasm shown for this petition, along with the poor turnout at the march the previous week, showed that, even though there was a lack of trust in the Ibrox board, there was just as little trust in the rebel faction.

It's a serious dilemma that faces The People; do they want money-men at their new club or do the want 'Real Rangers Men'? By the looks of things, they might not be able to have both. Keeping the Big Lie going is the most important issue ever to face The People and their friends in the media and, as we have seen, having 'Real Rangers Men' at the top of the marble staircase would go some way toward convincing themselves, if not everyone else, that Rangers never died. Clearing out the ones that own and run the club at present is paramount; they're a constant reminder of the realities of liquidation. Unfortunately, if those individuals and companies go, then they'll take their money with them.

A skint, kid-on 'Rangers' or a new club with, if not untold wealth, at least enough money to keep going; which one do they want? The agnivores are pinning their hopes on Dave King as being able to provide both. But can The People trust a convicted criminal and proven liar? And the agnivores hardly have a great record when it comes to hitching their star to a 'billionaire'. It's hardly a great choice. You almost feel sorry for them.

Then again, as things stand, they don't have a choice at all. They don't count skulls at AGMs; they count shares. The People certainly don't have the power to change anything at Neo-Gers, so their friends in the Scottish media are going all out to try to get the investors to change sides. They're not using the technique of persuasive argument, however; all they're doing is constantly sniping at the Neo-Gers board, painting all its members in a negative light.

The cloak-and-dagger investors aren't going to like all this publicity and the hope is that they'll be forced into having to abandon the current administration. It's a dangerous game to play, since the investors might well decide to just cut their losses.

Of course, the argument of King and his entourage is that Neo-Gers is already skint, having pissed away £70million in the past two years. These financial arguments, however, are nothing but rationalisations of the real reason for the anti-board rhetoric. This is easily seen through the fact that nobody among King's supporters, either among The People or the agnivores, will point any finger of blame at Sooperally, even though he's been bleeding the club dry as much as anyone. It's a straight, or, given the stance of the media, a not-so-straight, fight between new-club money and the 'Real Rangers Men'.

So what's going to happen next in this stalemate? Well, The People are going to be in for a major shock if Neo-Gers doesn't manage to pull in enough cash. Administration and even liquidation are a distinct possibility, if not probability. Those institutional investors aren't going to just sit around waiting to see if things improve; the hedge funds especially
have their own investors to worry about. And this time, things would be done properly.

If, as many folk think, Dave King is looking to cause insolvency so he can pick up the whole shebang on the cheap, then he's in for a nasty surprise. The creditors this time around aren't in the paper-shop and face-painter category; these characters are serious money men. They couldn't give two shits about 'Rangers' and its history or whatever; all they're interested in is figures in the credit column. If nobody's going to buy season books and the share price stays down, then it's time to cut the losses and get rid.

Sooperally and his team are supposedly off for a tour of North America soon, despite the lack of cash.[8] Presumably the American contingent of the global fan-base will be putting the players up in their homes. Even if they manage to scrape the money together to make this tour a reality, the chances are that they won't have a team to come back to.

Mind you, we've all been wrong about this before and we've seen all the stops pulled out by our football authorities to make sure that there's still a 'Rangers' for the People to follow follow. But this time could be different. Laxey, Margarita, Blue Pitch and the rest won't be satisfied with some put-up job as happened in 2012. I really can't see how they're going to weasel out of this one. But, as I say, we've all been wrong before. Whatever happens to the stadium or Murray Park I'm sure our authorities, and our media, will still be banging on about 'Rangers,' even if it's a team playing their home games on a pitch marked out at Elder Park! As long as there's somebody running the team that knows the words to 'The Sash' and has no doubts about the Big Lie, i.e. a 'Real Rangers Man' then nothing else matters.

Conclusion
Lost in the Supermarket

In a couple of years' time we could yet see a themed Asda superstore where Ibrox Stadium once was. The façade is a listed building so that will probably be the front of the store. A huge sign will announce, 'We Are The People – for low, low prices!' Another will say, 'Value then, Value now, Value forever!' Meanwhile a fleet of home-delivery vans can be seen, all bearing the slogan on their sides, 'We're coming down the road!'

Inside, the theme continues. You can get quality meat at the 'Succulent Lamb' butchers' counter, bread at the Broonloaf Stand and a pint of milk at Dairy's Wall. Over at the sports' department there are old Rangers tops for that retro look, while the Bill Struth section sells boating accessories. At the checkout there are leaflets offering EBT loans and you can sign up for the 'Rangers Loyal' loyalty card.

Okay, I'm probably talking shite here, but the chances of this happening are now higher than ever. We might actually get to a stage where our media accept, finally, that Rangers is dead. I wouldn't hold my breath, though. Even if they have to stick blue shirts and five stars on the Govan High School football team, the agnivores in our press will find something to call 'Rangers'!

Anyway, what have we learned from all this stuff? If you ask The People you'll soon discover that they've learnt nothing; they're still living in some imaginary world where they're God's Chosen and their team is the biggest, most-successful team on the planet, despite all evidence to the contrary. 'We Are The People' is still their cry and anything that goes wrong is down to an envious, hate-filled, bigoted conspiracy.

For the rest of us, the big discovery was how desperate the need was for these people to have some kind of focus in their lives. Brought up to believe in their innate superiority they've watched all the reasons for this belief disappear. Britain is no longer a world power, the Empire has disappeared and Reformed

Protestantism is not the only game in town anymore, nor does it profess to be. Power-sharing is being attempted in Northern Ireland and Catholics in this country are no longer second-class citizens. With all the things they took for granted gone it's no wonder they clung to the corpse of their team; it was all they had left.

Like Victor Frankenstein they reanimated the corpse but, unlike the famous fictional doctor, they pretended that the monster was still the same person as one of those that had involuntarily donated their body parts; presumably it was whoever's arse was stitched on!

The Big Lie that said that Rangers hadn't died and that Green's new club was still Rangers led to two predictable consequences. The first was that since The People saw it as still Rangers then they expected it to act like Rangers. That included spending like the old club. Items like the big, shiny, new, sooper-dooper team bus were a justifiable expense for 'Scotland's biggest club'. Also justifiable was the second-highest wage bill in Scotland to win a league against part-timers. They had to build for the future, for when they got back to their 'rightful place at the top' was the excuse. And so they follow-followed, not asking about how much money was being spent and blasting anyone that made negative noises as being a 'Rangers hater'.

Of course, asking no questions about the money meant that when The People finally found out the truth it came as a major shock. But, really, what else did they expect? They had been happy enough to go along with the dodgy deal between Duff and Phelps and Charles Green to shaft all the creditors. It shouldn't have come as a surprise to find that the same folk were out to fleece them as well!

The other consequence was the call for 'Real Rangers Men' to be in charge at Ibrox. This was a predictable outcome of the Big Lie since it would obviously be seen as necessary for the pretence of continuity to have any value. Charlie Boy was alright as things went but he didn't have 'Rangers' in his heart, no matter how much he might say that he had caught 'Rangersitis'.

This call for 'Real Rangers Men' was entirely separate from the financial considerations. Both The Requisitioners and Dave King promised to spend, spend, spend and this was obviously what The People wanted. All the shouting about 'spivs' and 'crooks' in the boardroom was just a cover for their real aims. After all, they'd tried to get rid of Charlie almost as soon as he was in the door!

And so we've reached the impasse of the present day. The bedsheet wavers want their 'Real Rangers Man' to take over, even though he's a convicted crook and fraudster. The other side of the war wants the current board to remain, blaming the 'Real Rangers Men' for causing all the trouble in the first place.

Neither side looks to be winning while many have decided not to renew their season tickets for a variety of reasons; not least of which is the hopeless, hapless and helpless Sooperally. The Championship next year is being touted with claims that it's going to be the most exciting league in Scotland, with both Hearts and Hibs relegated. You'd hardly think so with the amount of Neo-Gers supporters keeping their hands in their pockets. Maybe they've finally come to accept the truth that Rangers is deceased and there's no going back.

The more likely explanation, however, is that the price of a season book has gone up and no doubt measures have now been put in place to stop adults buying juvenile tickets. That's the only time that financial considerations trump the need for 'Real Rangers Men' for The People; when it affects their own pockets!

One final thing that we learned from this debacle: when times are tough you need a laugh. Back in the 1930s everyone had George Formby and Arthur Askey, God help them! In the 1980s we had the alternative comedians, The Young Ones and Only Fools and Horses. Now, in today's desperate financial climate, we've had Rangers and Neo-Gers to make us laugh. I'll leave you to decide which decade has provided the best comedy.

NOTES

Chapter 1 Complete Control

[1]http://www.dailyrecord.co.uk/sport/football/rangers-crisis-singapore-bid-chief-1119468#SIPrwgwRuJqRS2c7.97

[2]http://www.dailymail.co.uk/sport/football/article-2132691/Rangers-crisis-Bill-Miller-favourite-Bill-Ng-withdraws.html

[3] ibid

[4]http://www.dailyrecord.co.uk/news/scottish-news/rangers-bid-millionaire-bill-miller-877154

[5]http://www.scotsman.com/news/uk/rangers-takeover-fans-against-us-tycoon-bill-miller-s-incubator-plan-1-2248790

[6]http://www.dailyrecord.co.uk/sport/football/rangers-in-crisis-ally-mccoist-set-1129214

[7]http://www.dailyrecord.co.uk/sport/football/walter-smith-i-heard-mate-crying-1129311

[8]http://www.dailyrecord.co.uk/sport/football/rangers-in-crisis-walter-smith-should-1129315

[9]http://www.dailyrecord.co.uk/sport/football/rangers-in-crisis-ibrox-fans-to-snub-1129316

[10]http://www.dailyrecord.co.uk/news/scottish-news/rangers-in-crisis-walter-smith-gutted-1129783

[11]http://www.dailyrecord.co.uk/sport/football/rangers-in-crisis-ally-mccoist-admits-1129414

[12]http://www.dailyrecord.co.uk/sport/football/james-traynor-spl-will-not-be-able-1129166

[13] http://www.dailyrecord.co.uk/sport/football/powerbrokers-have-known-of-rangers-ebts-for-years-1327563

[14] ibid

[15] http://davidleggat-leggoland.blogspot.co.uk/ 21st December 2012

[16] http://stv.tv/sport/football/clubs/rangers/205975-european-clubs-body-downgrades-rangers-status-but-recognises-history/

[17] ibid

[18] https://www.theguardian.com/media/greenslade/2012/sep/03/sun-scotland

[19] http://www.dailymail.co.uk/sport/football/article-2213109/Charles-Green defiant-winning-disrepute-case-SPL.html

Chapter 2 What's My Name

[1] http://www.dailyrecord.co.uk/sport/football/powerbrokers-have-known-of-rangers-ebts-for-years-1327563

[2] http://www.out-law.com/articles/2012/november/employee-benefit-trust-payments-to-rangers-staff-and-players-were-not-illegal-says-tribunal/

[3] http://www.dailyrecord.co.uk/sport/football/football-news/after-rangers-biggest-ever-win-1447935

[4] http://billmcmurdo.wordpress.com/ 21st November 2012

[5]http://www.dailyrecord.co.uk/sport/football/football-news/after-rangers-biggest-ever-win-1447935

[6] http://www.bbc.co.uk/news/uk-scotland-19556780

[7]http://www.dailyrecord.co.uk/news/scottish-news/disgraced-ex-rangers-owner-craig-whyte-1385032

[8]http://www.dailyrecord.co.uk/news/scottish-news/falkirk-take-action-over-pa-1270898

[9] McMurdo Op. Cit. 16th December 2012

Chapter 3 Give 'Em Enough Rope

[1] http://www.dailyrecord.co.uk/sport/football/crass-is-always-greener-1117659

[2] ibid

[3]http://www.dailyrecord.co.uk/sport/football/football-news/if-rangers-fans-want-a-panto-villain-1488998

[4]http://www.belfasttelegraph.co.uk/sport/football/scottish/hateley-tips-lafferty-to-blast-rangers-to-more-glory-28633831.html

[5]http://www.dailyrecord.co.uk/sport/football/football-news/after-rangers-biggest-ever-win-1447935

Chapter 4 Career Opportunities

[1] http://www.dailyrecord.co.uk/sport/football/spare-me-the-doc-and-bull-tales-974906

[2] http://celticparanoia.blogspot.co.uk/2008/05/james-traynor-shameless-two-faced.html

[3] http://www.bbc.co.uk/blogs/legacy/chickyoung/2008/08/chick_youngs_blog.html

[4] http://www.dailyrecord.co.uk/sport/football/stop-giving-it-a-ref-ear-988581

[5] http://www.dailyrecord.co.uk/sport/other-sports/rangers-boss-walter-smith-blasts-997626

[6] http://www.dailyrecord.co.uk/sport/other-sports/now-fuming-yogi-lets-rip-988480

[7] http://www.dailyrecord.co.uk/opinion/sport/league-reconstruction-is-back-on-the-agenda-of-scottish-1343608

[8] http://www.dailyrecord.co.uk/sport/football/football-news/if-hearts-go-down-watch-other-clubs-1424368

[9] http://www.dailyrecord.co.uk/sport/football/football-news/the-500k-question-why-did-hearts-ko-rangers-1431486

[10] http://www.dailyrecord.co.uk/sport/football/football-news/dundee-united-chief-stephen-thompson-1460684

[11] http://www.dailyrecord.co.uk/sport/football/football-news/james-traynor-why-this-is-my-last-ever-newspaper-1470050

[12] http://blogs.channel4.com/alex-thomsons-view/succulent-lamb-rack/4144

[13]http://www.dailyrecord.co.uk/sport/football/rangers-owner-craig-whyte-admits-1115406

[14]http://www.dailyrecord.co.uk/sport/football/football-news/keith-jackson-greens-boycott-call-1482796

Chapter 5 Hate and War

[1] http://forweonlyknow.wordpress.com/2012/10/11/chris-graham-rants/ This article is no longer there and I can find no other copy of 'Ze List' online, but see: https://thehoopsetter.wordpress.com/

[2] Leggat Op. Cit. 28th December 2012

[3]The original article seems to have disappeared, but see here for a taste: http://www.dailyrecord.co.uk/sport/football/football-news/celtic-charged-by-sfa-over-rangers-1334946

[4] Leggat had to delete a lot of his blogs, due to his habit of slandering people and giving out their addresses and phone numbers. There is a huge gap, therefore, in his archive pages. He claims, however, that his blog was hacked.

[5] Daily Record 20th September 2012. They subsequently changed this page but see: http://celticunderground.net/which-banner-have-the-sfa-based-their-charges-on/

[6]http://www.dailyrecord.co.uk/sport/football/football-news/time-jim-was-on-gardening-leave-1363060

[7] Leggat Op. Cit. 28th December 2012

[8]http://news.stv.tv/west-central/105837-rangers-liquidation-now-inevitable-after-cva-bid-rejected-by-hmrc/

[9] http://www.bbc.co.uk/sport/0/football/20595802

Chapter 6 Guns On The Roof

[1]http://www.dailymail.co.uk/news/article-1326063/Jon-Snow-poppy-fascism-row-C4-News-host-refuses-surrender.html

[2]http://www.telegraph.co.uk/news/uknews/9629864/Poppy-fascism-row-reignites-over-accusations-appeal-has-been-hijacked-by-politicians-and-B-list-celebrities.html

[3] https://www.theguardian.com/uk/2012/oct/15/royal-british-legion-president-quits

[4]http://www.dailymail.co.uk/sport/football/article-2231071/James-McClean-refuses-wear-poppy.html

[5] McMurdo Op. Cit. 9th November 2013

[6] ibid 12th November 2013

[7]http://www.dailyrecord.co.uk/news/scottish-news/rangers-remembrance-day-parade-branded-1558062

[8] ibid

[9] ibid

[10] ibid

[11]http://www.theshedend.com/topic/22781-now-we-cannot-even-support-our-troops-in-scotland/

[12] http://forum.rangersmedia.co.uk/index.php?showtopic=246577

Chapter 7 Cheapskates

[1] http://www.bbc.co.uk/sport/0/football/20292601

[2]http://www.dailyrecord.co.uk/news/scottish-news/rangers-in-crisis-walter-smith-gutted-1129783

[3] McMurdo Op. Cit. 13th December 2012

[4]http://www.dailyrecord.co.uk/sport/football/football-news/charles-green-on-the-backfoot-for-first-time-1493627

[5] Leggat Op. Cit. 21st December 2012

[6] http://rangers.co.uk/news/headlines/rangers-listed-on-london-stock-exchange/

[7] http://www.bbc.co.uk/news/uk-scotland-glasgow-west-20773142

Chapter 8 Hateful

[1]http://www.dailyrecord.co.uk/sport/football/football-news/silent-majority-need-to-rise-up-1512272

[2] Leggat Op. Cit. 28th December 2012

[3] http://www.rangers.co.uk/news/opinion/item/3316-time-for-fans-to-unite

[4] http://www.rangers.co.uk/news/opinion/item/3085-remember-sporting-integrity?

[5] ibid

[6] http://rangers.co.uk/news/headlines/well-are-welcome/

[7] ibid

[8] http://www.dailyrecord.co.uk/sport/football/football-news/dundee-united-fans-have-a-cheek-to-attack-1475500

[9] http://www.dailyrecord.co.uk/sport/football/football-news/keith-jackson-greens-boycott-call-1482796

[10] http://www.dailyrecord.co.uk/sport/football/football-news/tam-cowan-charles-green-needs-1479139

[11] http://www.dailyrecord.co.uk/sport/football/football-news/rangers-fans-angry-at-dundee-united-1552600

[12] http://www.scotzine.com/2013/02/rangers-supporters-assembly-vp-tenders-resignation-after-flouting-united-boycott/

Chapter 9 Justice Tonight

[1] http://www.dailyrecord.co.uk/sport/football/football-news/mark-hateley-fear-future-game-1734774

[2]http://www.dailyrecord.co.uk/sport/football/football-news/spl-fight-to-strip-rangers-of-league-1447930

[3]http://www.eveningtimes.co.uk/sport/13255088.Hateley__Get_Gers_back_in_the_SPL_now/

[4] ibid

[5]http://www.dailyrecord.co.uk/sport/football/football-news/rangers-boss-ally-mccoist-not-1740534

[6]http://www.dailyrecord.co.uk/sport/football/football-news/sports-hotline-friday-march-1-1736670

[7] McMurdo Op. Cit. 21st November 2012

Chapter 10 Something About England

[1]http://www.dailyrecord.co.uk/sport/football/rangers-richer-than-celtic-in-a-year-says-1190504

[2] ibid

[3]http://www.dailyrecord.co.uk/sport/football/rangers-in-crisis-charles-green-insists-1128972

[4]http://www.dailyrecord.co.uk/sport/football/football-news/rangers-chief-charles-green-set-1335458

[5] http://www.bbc.co.uk/news/uk-scotland-scotland-business-21621106

[6]http://www.dailyrecord.co.uk/sport/football/football-

news/rangers-chief-charles-green-set-1335458

[7]http://www.scotzine.com/2012/11/the-phantom-commercial-partnership-between-rangers-and-dallas-cowboys/

[8]http://www.dailyrecord.co.uk/sport/football/football-news/rangers-chief-charles-green-i-wont-1497900

[9]http://www.dailymail.co.uk/sport/football/article-2224771/Rangers-wont-play-SPL-watch-says-Charles-Green.html

[10]http://www.independent.co.uk/sport/football/news-and-comment/rangers-we-want-to-play-in-england-8323898.html

[11] ibid

[12]http://www.scotsman.com/sport/football/competitions/english/manchester-united-reject-charles-green-s-claim-they-want-rangers-in-england-1-2641708

[13]http://www.dailyrecord.co.uk/sport/football/rangers-are-being-bullied-out-of-scotland-1542827

[14] Leggat

[15]https://scotslawthoughts.wordpress.com/2013/02/01/deja-vu-all-over-again-reaction to the-sfa-arbitration-panels-rejection-of-rangers-claim/

Chapter 11 Play To Win

[1] http://forum.rangersmedia.co.uk/index.php?showtopic=237640

[2] ibid

[3] ibid

[4]http://www.dailyrecord.co.uk/sport/football/tam-cowan-rangers-crossbar-challenge-1311382

[5]http://scotslawthoughts.wordpress.com/2013/05/06/red-card-warning-for-rangers-1-million-competition-by-ecojon/

[6] ibid

[7]http://forum.rangersmedia.co.uk/index.php?showtopic=237640

[8] https://www.youtube.com/watch?v=VFV-OFFpqeY

Chapter 12 Should I Stay Or Should I Go

[1] http://www.dailyrecord.co.uk/incoming/rangers-chief-charles-green-tells-1819472

[2]http://sport.stv.tv/football/clubs/rangers/219860-rangers-chief-scout-neil-murray-has-left-the-club-after-an-investigation/

[3] http://www.rangers.co.uk/news/headlines/item/3629-yeates-leaves-rangers

[4]http://www.dailymail.co.uk/sport/football/article-2296206/Rangers-star-Francisco-Sandaza-duped-Celtic-fan-cabbie-astonishing-23-minute-phonecall--listen-clip.html

[5]http://www.dailyrecord.co.uk/sport/football/football-news/charles-green-threatens-walk-unless-1717127

[6] http://www.bbc.co.uk/news/uk-scotland-glasgow-west-19976991

[7]http://www.dailyrecord.co.uk/news/scottish-news/craig-whytes-secret-court-documents-1814591

[8]http://www.dailyrecord.co.uk/news/scottish-news/rangers-boardroom-war-hits-new-1901882

[9]http://paddyontherailway12.blogspot.co.uk/2013/05/film-2013-while-rich-and-famous-are.html

[10] McMurdo Op. Cit. 30th May 2013

[11] Leggat Op. Cit. 31st May 2013

[12]http://www.dailyrecord.co.uk/sport/football/football-news/keith-jackson-d-day-hearts-scottish-1900036

Chapter 13 Police And Thieves

[1] Leggat Op. Cit. 16th May 2013

[2] ibid 14th May 2013

[3] McMurdo Op. Cit. 16th May 2013

[4]http://www.dailyrecord.co.uk/sport/football/football-news/rangers-takeover-tapes-reveal-secret-1997376

[5] ibid

[6] ibid

[7] Ibid

Chapter 14 Lightning Strikes

[1]http://www.dailyrecord.co.uk/sport/football/football-news/hearts-crisis-battle-tynecastle-underway-1960586

[2] McMurdo Op. Cit. 19th June 2013

[3] ibid

[4]http://blogs.channel4.com/alex-thomsons-view/political-interference-scottish-football/1134

[5] http://www.bbc.co.uk/sport/0/football/23595820

[6]http://www.dailyrecord.co.uk/opinion/sport/hotline/sports-hotline-rangers-fans-vent-1989397

[7] McMurdo Op. Cit. 21st June 2013

[8] ibid 19th June 2013

[9]http://www.telegraph.co.uk/sport/football/teams/hearts/10146384/Hearts-manager-Gary-Locke-tells-Rangers-fans-we-dont-need-your-help.html

[10] McMurdo Op. Cit. 19th June 2013

Chapter 15 48 Hours

[1] Leggat Op. Cit. 30th July 2013

[2]http://www.dailyrecord.co.uk/sport/football/football-news/keith-jackson-monday-june-3-1928493

[3] McMurdo Op. Cit. 31st July 2013

[4]http://www.dailyrecord.co.uk/sport/football/football-news/dundee-united-chief-stephen-thompson-1460684

[5]http://www.dailyrecord.co.uk/sport/football/football-news/former-rangers-chief-executive-charles-2117643

[6]http://www.dailyrecord.co.uk/news/scottish-news/walter-smith-resigns-rangers-chairman-2127996

[7] ibid

[8] http://www.bbc.co.uk/sport/0/football/23268025

[9]http://www.dailymail.co.uk/sport/football/article-2384102/Charles-Green-Ally-McCoist-win-league-cup-double.html

[10]http://www.dailyrecord.co.uk/sport/football/football-news/rangers-boss-ally-mccoist-blasts-1817685

[11]http://www.dailyrecord.co.uk/sport/football/football-news/top-lawman-donald-findlay-warns-2128875

Chapter 16 Garageland

[1]http://www.scotsman.com/sport/football/teams/rangers/rangers-show-off-new-state-of-the-art-bus-1-2982214

[2]http://www.express.co.uk/news/uk/416282/Blaze-thugs-target-

Rangers-plush-new-coach

[3] McMurdo Op. Cit. 1st October 2013

[4]http://www.dailyrecord.co.uk/sport/football/football-news/bill-gates-could-running-rangers-2333671

[5]http://forum.rangersmedia.co.uk/index.php?/topic/259263-david-leggat-the-blue-pitch-and-margarita-mystery-continues/&page=1

Chapter 17 Deny

[1] http://www.bbc.co.uk/sport/0/football/24395665

[2]http://www.dailymail.co.uk/sport/football/article-2456882/Dave-King-ready-Rangers-chairman-positive-talks-South-Africa.html

[3]http://www.scotsman.com/sport/football/teams/rangers/dave-king-bids-to-be-rangers-chairman-1-3139572

[4]http://stv.tv/news/scotland/237753-dave-king-settles-on-44m-bill-with-south-african-authorities/

[5]http://www.fin24.com/Economy/Dave-King-must-pay-R706m-or-face-prison-20130829

[6]http://www.dailyrecord.co.uk/sport/football/football-news/rangers-power-struggle-am-fit-2666843

[7]http://www.dailyrecord.co.uk/sport/football/football-news/hugh-keevins-peter-lawwell-casting-2365795

[8]http://www.express.co.uk/sport/football/440226/Celtic-s-Peter-Lawwell-won-t-vote-on-ex-Rangers-director-Dave-King

[9]http://www.dailyrecord.co.uk/news/scottish-news/ibrox-chief-craig-mather-walks-2461157

[10] http://www.bbc.co.uk/sport/football/24775751

Chapter 18 Remote Control

[1]http://www.followfollow.com/news/tmnw/orange_order_sells_shares_in_rangers_to_members_and_supporters_160789/index.shtml

[2] http://www.dailyrecord.co.uk/sport/football/all-mouth-and-rouser-1269998

[3] http://www.bbc.co.uk/sport/0/football/19376352

Chapter 19 Hitsville UK

[1] McMurdo Op. Cit. 13th November 2013

[2] ibid 15th December 2012

[3] ibid

[4] ibid 22nd December 2013

[5] ibid 10th January 2014

[6] ibid 15th November 2013

[7] ibid 13th 2013

[8] ibid 30th November 2013

Chapter 20 Last Gang in Town

[1]https://www.facebook.com/SonsOfStruth#!/SonsOfStruth/info

[2] http://tfk.thefreekick.com/t/bill-struth-facts/21509

[3]http://www.dailyrecord.co.uk/sport/football/football-news/battle-rangers-fan-behind-sons-2913943

[4] McMurdo Op. Cit. 18th November 2013

[5] Leggat Op. Cit. 18th November 2013

Chapter 21 Four Horsemen

[1]http://www.dailyrecord.co.uk/sport/football/football-news/rebel-paul-murray-wants-know-2786527

[2]http://www.express.co.uk/sport/football/440422/Jim-McColl-I-have-the-finance-to-take-Rangers-forward

[3] Leggat Op. Cit. 2nd December 2013

[4]http://www.dailyrecord.co.uk/sport/football/football-news/keith-jackson-ibrox-whistleblowers-must-2874396

[5] ibid

[6]http://www.dailyrecord.co.uk/sport/football/football-news/keith-jackson-burger-van-fiasco-2932359

Chapter 22 Safe European Home

[1]http://www.dailyrecord.co.uk/sport/football/football-news/rebel-paul-murray-wants-know-2786527

[2]http://www.dailyrecord.co.uk/sport/football/football-news/rebel-paul-murray-wants-know-2786527

[3]http://www.dailyrecord.co.uk/sport/football/football-news/internal-investigation-rangers-set-clear-1910095

[4]http://www.dailymail.co.uk/sport/football/article-2523948/Malcolm-Murray-insists-Rangers-need-cleaning--exclusive.html

[5] http://www.thecoplandroad.org/2013/11/exclusive-cro-talks-with-paul-murray.html

Chapter 23 The Equaliser

[1] http://www.parliament.uk/search/results/?q=180784

[2]http://www.publications.parliament.uk/pa/cm201314/cmhansrd/cm140106/text/140106w0006.htm

Chapter 24 The Clampdown

[1]http://www.telegraph.co.uk/news/uknews/1358985/Sept-11-a-good-day-to-bury-bad-news.html

[2] Leggat Op. Cit. 18th November 2013

[3]http://www.dailyrecord.co.uk/news/scottish-news/rangers-director-brian-stockbridge-splashed-2464822

[4] The picture has disappeared but see McMurdo Op. Cit. 23rd October 2013

[5]http://www.dailyrecord.co.uk/sport/football/football-news/celtic-wont-face-action-over-2839975

Chapter 25 Know Your Rights

[1] McMurdo Op. Cit. 10th October 2013

[2] Leggat Op. Cit. 16th December 2013

[3] http://www.bbc.co.uk/sport/0/football/24395665

[4]http://www.dailyrecord.co.uk/sport/football/football-news/rangers-chief-executive-graham-wallace-2935620

[5]http://www.dailyrecord.co.uk/sport/football/football-news/ally-mccoist-hailed-rangers-fans-2935560

[6] Leggat Op. Cit. 16th December 2013

[7]http://www.dailyrecord.co.uk/sport/football/football-news/rangers-agm-paul-murray-issues-2942074

Chapter 26 One More Time

[1]http://www.dailyrecord.co.uk/sport/football/football-news/rangers-players-refuse-accept-15-3029838

[2]http://www.dailyrecord.co.uk/sport/football/football-news/rangers-pay-cut-shock-exclusive-3030771

[3]http://blogs.channel4.com/alex-thomsons-view/red-whyte-blue-rangers-saga-continues/7119

[4] McMurdo Op. Cit. 31st January 2014

[5]http://www.dailyrecord.co.uk/sport/football/football-news/rangers-bring-new-financial-guru-3009812

[6]http://www.dailyrecord.co.uk/sport/football/football-news/guernsey-based-hedge-fund-damille-investments-3027112

[7]https://www.youtube.com/watch?v=o5TAmH9bMs4

[8]http://www.dailyrecord.co.uk/sport/football/football-news/manager-ally-mccoist-launches-defence-3042744

[9] ibid

[10]http://forum.rangersmedia.co.uk/index.php?/topic/264055-no-more-turnberry/&page=2

[11]http://www.dailyrecord.co.uk/sport/football/football-transfer-news/rangers-boot-out-900k-nottingham-3087772

[12]http://www.dailyrecord.co.uk/sport/football/football-transfer-

news/rangers-boss-ally-mccoist-reveals-3128460

[13] http://dothebouncy.com/main/threads/a-bit-cheeky-of-barry-ferguson.59684/

[14] http://www.dailyrecord.co.uk/sport/football/football-news/the-500k-question-why-did-hearts-ko-rangers-1431486

[15] http://www.express.co.uk/sport/football/455918/Brian-Stockbridge-leaves-Rangers

[16] http://www.dailyrecord.co.uk/sport/football/football-news/keith-jackson-dave-king-ready-3065509

[17] ibid

[18] http://www.dailyrecord.co.uk/sport/football/football-news/rangers-agm-rebels-routed-ibrox-2945203#2YCPuqfUZshX2m75.97

Chapter 27 Movers and Shakers

[1] http://www.heraldscotland.com/sport/13126993.Stockbridge__Rangers_will_be_down_to_last___1m_by_April/

[2] http://www.dailyrecord.co.uk/sport/football/football-news/rangers-chief-executive-graham-wallace-3046934

[3] http://www.dailyrecord.co.uk/sport/football/football-news/rangers-confirm-15million-loan-sandy-3178518

[4] http://www.bbc.co.uk/sport/football/26333152

[5] http://www.bbc.co.uk/sport/football/26358424

[6] ibid

[7] http://www.iol.co.za/business/news/tax-court-labels-king-shameless-glib-liar-1.1027561

[8] http://www.bbc.co.uk/sport/football/26366511

[9] ibid

[10] http://www.bdlive.co.za/articles/2008/11/11/king-s-tax-assessment-valid---sars

[11] http://www.bbc.co.uk/sport/football/26358424

[12] http://www.dailyrecord.co.uk/sport/football/football-news/keith-jackson-time-come-dave-3190897

[13] http://www.dailyrecord.co.uk/sport/football/football-news/rangers-manager-ally-mccoist-refuses-3193342

[14] http://www.dailyrecord.co.uk/sport/football/football-news/keith-jackson-time-come-dave-3190897

[15] McMurdo Op. Cit. 28th February 2014

Chapter 28 The Right Profile

[1] http://dothebouncy.com/main/threads/sons-of-struth-shut-down.59252/

[2] http://www.dailyrecord.co.uk/sport/football/football-news/rangers-fans-claim-been-hit-3232161

[3] ibid

[4]http://www.dailyrecord.co.uk/sport/football/football-news/sandy-easdales-lawyers-threaten-sue-3239928

[5]http://www.eveningtimes.co.uk/news/13275850.Rangers_end_relationship_with_Jack_Irvine_s_PR_firm/

[6] http://www.totrust.co.za/20131122_jse.html

[7]http://www.dailyrecord.co.uk/sport/football/football-news/dave-king-accuses-rangers-board-3254816

[8]http://www.dailyrecord.co.uk/sport/football/football-news/rangers-supporters-vow-press-season-3258837

[9] McMurdo Op. Cit. 31st March 2014

[10]http://www.dailyrecord.co.uk/sport/football/football-news/rangers-fan-caught-legal-battle-3276483

[11] http://dothebouncy.com/main/threads/fuckin-easdales-actin-like-tims.60291/

[12]http://www.gersnetonline.co.uk/vb/showthread.php?62784-Easdale-suing-Craig-Houston-SOS

[13] McMurdo Op. Cit. 31st March 2014

[14]http://www.dailyrecord.co.uk/sport/football/football-news/keith-jackson-celtic-charge-10-in-a-row-3294152

[15]http://www.dailyrecord.co.uk/sport/football/football-news/keith-jackson-its-matter-trust-3303691

Chapter 29 Time Is Tight

[1]http://www.eveningtimes.co.uk/sport/13278100.Rangers_fans_pon der_ next_move_on_season_ticket_trust_fund/

[2]http://www.dailyrecord.co.uk/sport/football/football-news/rangers-power-struggle-union-fans-3415026

[3]http://www.dailyrecord.co.uk/sport/football/football-news/rangers-fans-fury-after-ally-3387132

[4]http://www.dailyrecord.co.uk/sport/football/football-news/sports-hotline-rangers-fans-line-3395025

[5]http://www.dailyrecord.co.uk/sport/football/football-news/rangers-boss-ally-mccoist-defiant-3403247

[6] http://www.bbc.co.uk/sport/football/26763952

[7]http://www.dailyrecord.co.uk/sport/football/football-news/rangers-power-struggle-union-fans-3415026

[8] http://rangers.co.uk/news/club/season-ticket-information/

[9]http://www.dailyrecord.co.uk/sport/football/football-news/outspoken-new-spin-doctor-rolls-3449016

Chapter 30 The Call Up

[1] McMurdo Op. Cit. 25th April 2014

[2]http://www.dailymail.co.uk/sport/football/article-2588429/Dave-King-commit-30m-ensure-Rangers-return-Scottish-Premiership.html

[3] ibid

[4] http://www.bbc.co.uk/sport/football/27353974

[5]http://www.dailyrecord.co.uk/sport/football/football-news/rangers-board-attacks-ibrox-1972-3503598

[6] McMurdo Op. Cit. 10th May 2014

[7]http://www.thescottishsun.co.uk/scotsol/homepage/sport/spl/4369672/Culprits-must-pay-price-after-killing-off-my-club.html

[8]http://www.dailyrecord.co.uk/sport/football/football-news/rangers-board-attacks-ibrox-1972-3503598

[9]http://www.dailyrecord.co.uk/sport/football/football-news/ready-listen-twitter-qa-rangers-3518435#3gDiZsSvSGC2gDbl.97

[10] ibid

[11]http://www.dailyrecord.co.uk/sport/football/football-news/gary-ralston-ibrox-chief-graham-3520635#WwgWqW7l87AB0GWz.97

[12] http://www.dailyrecord.co.uk/sport/football/alex-mcleish-rangers-fans-gone-3506048

[13]http://www.dailyrecord.co.uk/sport/football/football-news/rangers-legend-lorenzo-amoruso-backs-3525138

[14] http://www.dailyrecord.co.uk/sport/football/football-news/rangers-power-struggle-nacho-novo-3579575

[15]http://www.dailyrecord.co.uk/sport/football/football-news/former-rangers-defender-john-brown-3537543

[16] McMurdo Op. Cit. 19th May 2014

Chapter 31 Police On My Back

[1]http://www.dailyrecord.co.uk/sport/football/football-news/police-probe-launched-after-rangers-3464370

[2] ibid

[3]http://www.dailyrecord.co.uk/sport/football/football-news/keith-jackson-graham-wallace-man-3467717

[4]http://www.dailyrecord.co.uk/sport/football/football-news/rangers-face-second-police-probe-3592006

[5] ibid

[6] http://www.bbc.co.uk/sport/football/27353974

[7]http://www.dailyrecord.co.uk/sport/football/football-news/rangers-director-sandy-easdale-new-3580533

[8] http://www.dailyrecord.co.uk/sport/football/football-news/new-crisis-rangers-over-season-3604574

[9] https://www.ibrox1972.co.uk/ This website appears to have vanished.

[10] McMurdo Op. Cit. 24th May 2014

Chapter 32 The Street Parade

[1]http://www.heraldscotland.com/sport/13162143.400_Rangers_fans_in_Ibrox_protest/

[2] http://www.bbc.co.uk/sport/football/27558236

[3] https://www.youtube.com/watch?v=9s7jUFmiTes

[4]http://www.dailyrecord.co.uk/sport/football/football-news/battle-rangers-ibrox-board-brink-3544079

[5] McMurdo Op. Cit. 19th May 2014

[6]http://www.dailyrecord.co.uk/sport/football/football-news/rangers-fans-urged-not-buy-3549042

[7]http://www.dailyrecord.co.uk/sport/football/football-news/rangers-supporters-increase-pressure-under-fire-3629107

[8]http://www.rangers.vitalfootball.co.uk/article.asp?a=543511

Printed in Great Britain
by Amazon